Page		Content
3		Starting Point
14	1	A Global Issue
20	1.1	World Calculation Models
32	2	Stimulants
42	3	Recipes
52	4	Life Cycle Analysis
64	5	Universal Tools
70	5.1	A Recipe for an LCA
78	5.2	A Bold Life Cycle Analysis
80	6	Coffee Box
96	7	Quick Death
112	8	Long Life
122	9	Resurrection
134	10	Greenwashing
140	11	Creativity Tools
148	12	Offending the Audience
156	13	A Personal Matter
162	14	How Should We Live?
172	15	Future Concepts
178		Glossary
182		References and Recommended Reading
189		List of Illustrations of the IDRV's Activities
191		Agents

**Institute of
Design Research
Vienna**

Starting Point

Proclamation

We are designers, but also non-designers, autodidacts, researchers, specialists, experts in the design knowledge of the future. We have acquired this knowledge through research, through the learning process, through self-experimentation, through experimental approaches and through practice, but above all, we have acquired it in exchanges with other designers, autodidacts, researchers, specialists, students and experts. The knowledge that we want to share is therefore an associative universe of references – and not a linear thought pattern.

In this book, and in our work, we claim the right to challenge social contexts, but without making a direct political demand. From the standpoint of design, we formulate a radical critique of the existing structures that hinder sustainable lifestyles. We call for a fundamental revision of the role of design towards a democratization of design, and search for new forms of participation in design processes.

We call for the design revolution and we arm ourselves with calculators and hammers – both literally and with a good sense of humor – to take on an overpowering system. We are growing in number, and we want to confront the system with easy-to-use tools and knowledge-based tactics. Therefore, we use what is perhaps the most important role of design: communicating and visualizing complex relationships, pointing to and exploring other ways of acting and possible solutions. We want people who act autonomously and freely when it comes to raising their grievances; people who are confrontational – who refuse to put up with anything. People who might use our tools or develop others. We want to stimulate a change in thinking and begin to develop alternatives to the prevailing destructive lifestyles together.

Vienna 2014

Hammer

"Tool" is a metaphor for doing it yourself, for taking matters into your own hands. We do not want to believe anything but what we see for ourselves; we want to look at the insides of things and find out how something is made, and how something works. And above all, we want to start to do something on our own, and not wait until someone else starts to do something. This is what the hammer stands for. In its prototypical form as a hand ax, it is one of the oldest tools of humankind, which has changed only slightly in its design and not at all in its applicability. In its simplicity, it can be used by anyone – barrier-free, so to speak. In our case, it is a synonym for the analysis of objects and circumstances – for taking things apart, for seizing the initiative, for acting out on your own and for taking a stand; for subversive or direct resistance.

Cooking spoon

Like the hammer, the cooking spoon is an extension of the arm, but this time, it is a tool for stirring. In our case, it is emblematic of cooking for yourself. Taking action on your own is important here, too, but we see the spoon as a metaphor for synthesis – for assembling and linking the results. The next step after the hammer is made with a spoon, so to speak.

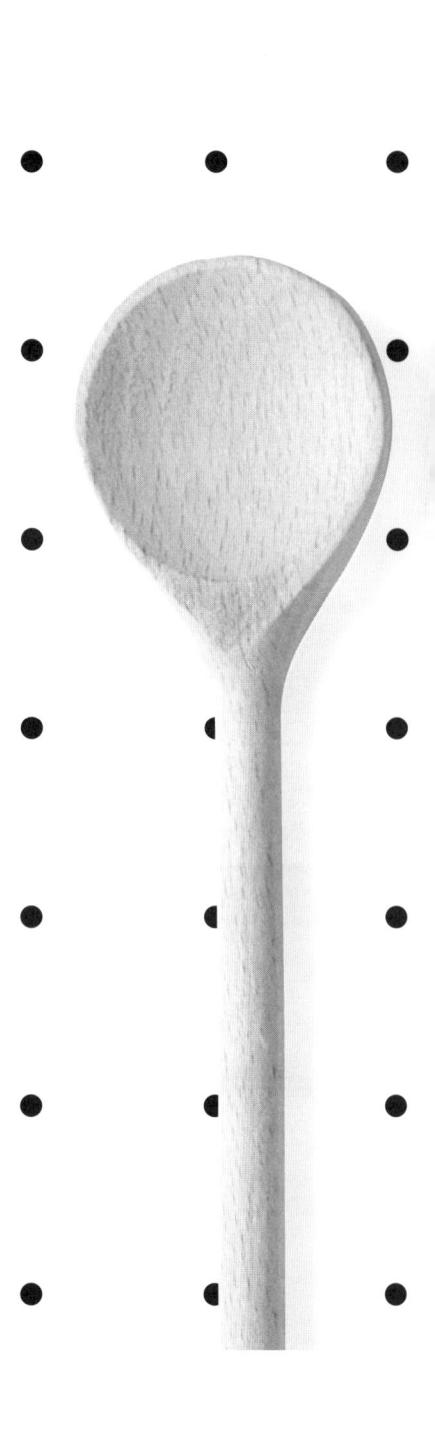

Tools for the Design Revolution

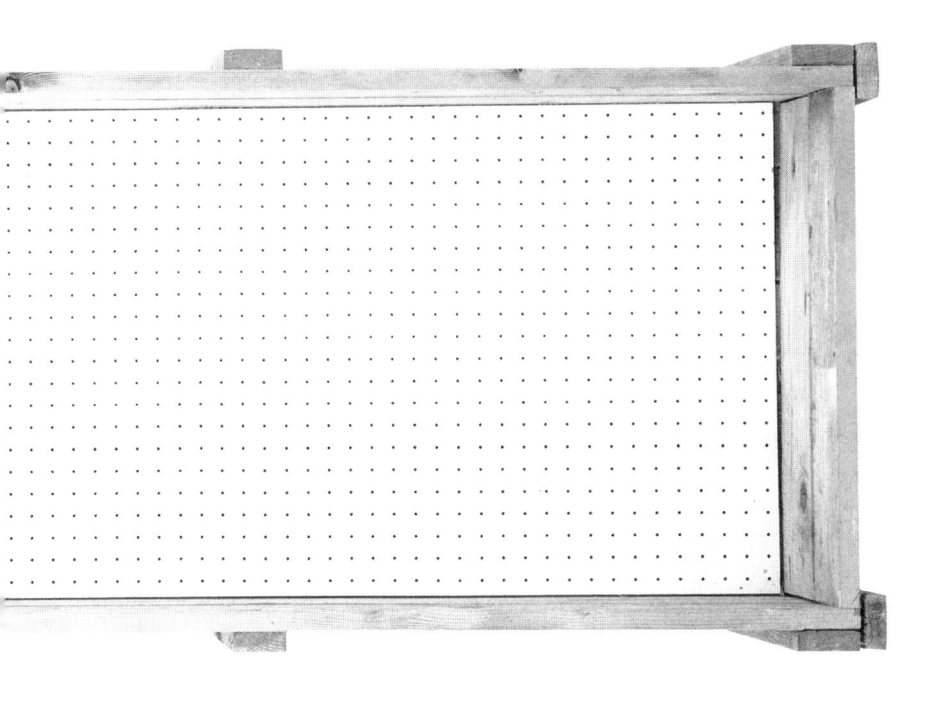

Tool box
As "tools", we have assembled not just the handheld mechanical devices that conform to a romantic notion of DIY, but also tools for thinking, methods for analysis or activism, self-empowering and enabling tools, as well as simple knowledge. Tools that introduce the possibility of taking action on your own into the complexity of the sustainability discourse.

The toolbox is the collection point for the tools of design revolution. Ordered, packaged, nicely labeled – there they are in their boxes, of which there are several: the box for life cycle analysis tools, the box for stimulants, the coffee box and so on. The boxes are like thinking spaces – small universes that specify a particular context. But they are not locked; they can be opened at any time, and the tools can be added to, rearranged or even reallocated.

Whole Earth Catalog
Like our toolboxes, the *Whole Earth Catalog* has assembled a variety of useful "tools" that can help the individual and the established community alike to make the world better for themselves and for others. This carefully curated compendium, first published in 1968 by Stewart Brand and reissued at irregular intervals until 1998, put on its cover the first image of Earth from outer space – our blue planet, floating alone in space, making it very clear that this is a self-contained ecosystem. This image of the Earth, like the *Whole Earth Catalog*, quickly became a symbol of the North American counterculture movement as well as the global environmental movement.

W H O

E A R

The catalog was intended as an aid for evaluating and visualizing useful things – an analog information system that anticipated the principles of digital search engines. But unlike the editors of the *Whole Earth Catalog*, who justified their choice of items with the statement "We only review stuff we think is great. Why waste your time on anything else?", we believe that it is also important to deal with things that have not been pre-selected, that are not a priori great, that are alien, that are still waiting to be discovered. We would be delighted if you wasted your time being curious, asking your own questions, looking things up, testing – and then sharing your knowledge.

L E

T H

Tools for the Design Revolution

Tools for the Design Revolution

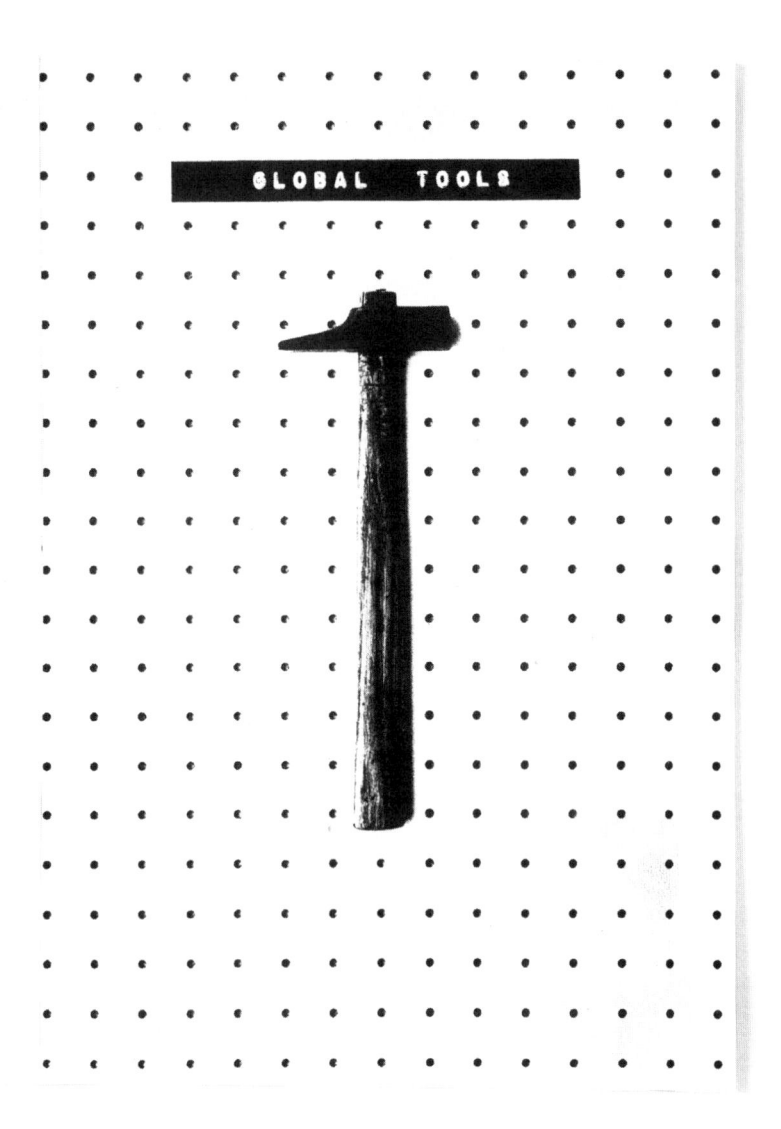

Global Tools

"Global Tools", which our section on the hammer referenced, was a loose, short-term consortium of Italian designers and architects that formed in 1973. In their eponymous magazine, they used as a cover image a hammer lying against the organizing element of a workshop cabinet – a pegboard, which, using the proper implements, can become a flexible ordering system. Global Tools saw themselves as communicative platform that experimented with the use of natural materials and traditional techniques in collective processes, and conveyed the results – as a counter-movement to industrial production. The goal was to promote the development of individual creativity. From today's perspective, this approach seems to be somewhat romantic, and yet it has currency: in the necessary appreciation of handcraft and its associated knowledge, which is increasingly being lost; in the aggregation of human competence; in dealing with natural materials (resources) and in the projection of responsibility onto each individual. The goal is not just to promote individual creativity; this has a stale aftertaste due to the neo-liberal agenda of the creative subject.

The goal is to empower each and every individual to act for him or herself, on his or her own initiative, in spite of the complexity of the sustainability discourse. The use of the tools for the design revolution is open to all – here, creativity is in demand again.

These are the t
Choose one.
Start the design revolut

ols.

n!

1

14 Tools for the Design Revolution

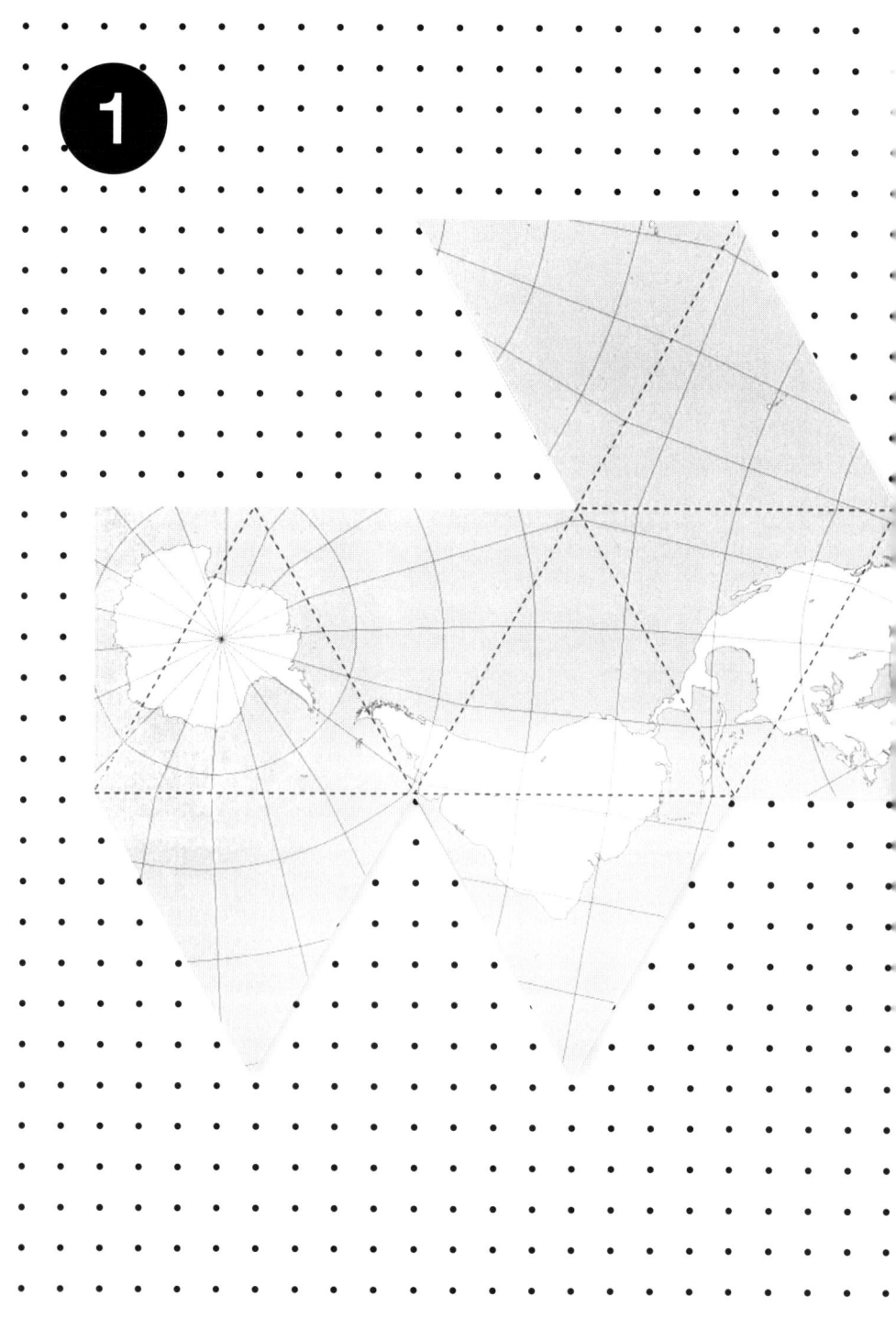

Tools for the Design Revolution

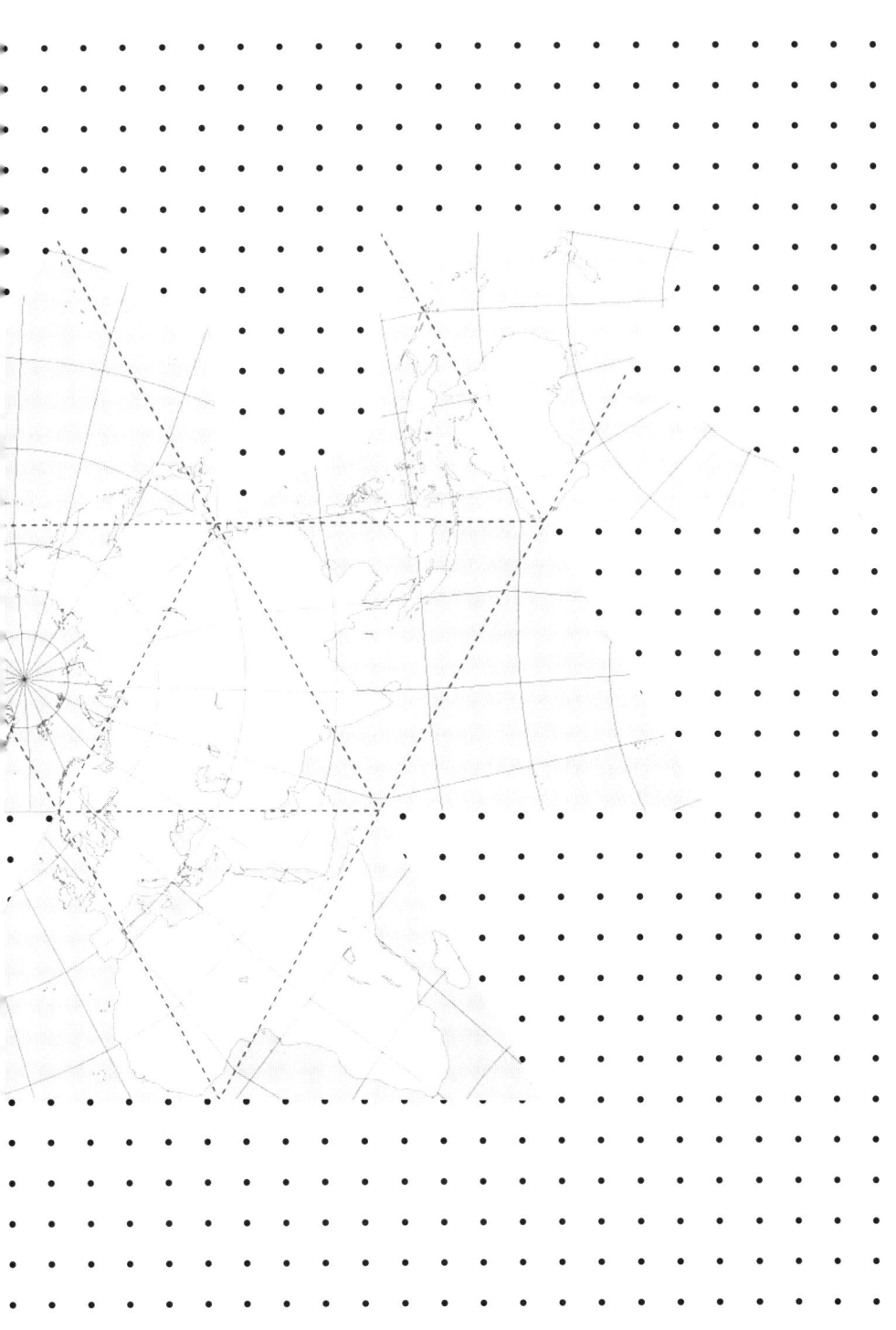

❶ A Global Issue

Hand luggage allowances for travel on Spaceship Earth

There are moments in which you ask yourself what you really need. But the trigger for this is not a philosophical question, a mid-life crisis or even a world crisis. No, it is a truly banal situation that brings us to this question, which is so important for survival on planet Earth: packing a piece of hand luggage.

Ironically, it is the very people who are suspected of having at least some responsibility for the economic misery of our day who deal with this world-important question of allowed hand luggage over and over. A curious social utopia: people who earn a thousand times or more than others actually engaging in self-limitation, every day. A metaphorical form of moderation in solidarity, with social implications. But the extent of this act of luggage solidarity is measured very precisely in cubic centimeters, as the monument to the largest possible amount of individually usable storage space in an aircraft can be found at any airport – in the form of that cage in which a real piece of luggage must fit at the request of the ground crew for the purpose of control.
If the hand luggage does not fit inside this shiny chrome tubular-steel sculpture, then the common journey of suitcase and passenger ends here. This problem can be circumvented by the acquisition of a suitable piece of luggage, which – no matter how much money you spend – always has the same dimensions. Even with the use of a platinum credit card, it can be no larger than 55 × 40 × 23 centimeters.

This little exercise in individual self-limitation could have revolutionary implications if it were transferred to people around the world – regardless of their origin or social status. Here, we practice the strategy for a solidarity-based, world-friendly lifestyle, where a radical limitation in the demands for individual space as well as energy applies to everyone. If the suitcase cannot be closed, we are not yet prepared for the new world – a world in which all restrictions would be as easy to describe as the dimensions for hand luggage. The key resources of the world are the limiting factors for our trip on Spaceship Earth. These factors include the biocapacity of the Earth, and global energy consumption.

The International Energy Agency publishes the amount of energy that the world consumes. If we take the available supply of energy and divide it by the number of people on Earth, we get another factor that, like the eight kilograms of hand luggage, limits our journey on the world: you can only consume about two thousand watts of continuous power per person.
If only this travel rule were applied to everyone, like the international hand luggage rule, then we would all live together on the Earth in solidarity, safety and comfort.
Unfortunately, not everyone follows it. The business class-traveling Europeans consume six thousand watts each, while the people in the United States actually consume twelve thousand. We only restrict the developing countries in this way; they are denied a pleasant stay on board.

Weight and dimensions are not the only rules designed to ensure safe transport for everyone. Dangerous things should also not be taken on board – another viable assumption for a sustainable lifestyle, not just above the clouds, but below as well. If you want to know how we should live in the future, you only have to read through the fine print on the boarding pass. No radioactive substances may be taken. Why? On the Earth, this is no problem; they just need to be well packed – about as well as the radioactive waste from nuclear power plants. Another example: carrying weapons is not allowed. Even if they fit in your pocket, the weapons could cause damage. It's better to be safe than sorry. Why is this not also true on the ground?

Gases are also prohibited. On the Earth, however, we are building new gas pipelines to satisfy our unbridled thirst for energy through supplies from countries that still have a long way to go towards democratization. And is gas not more environmentally friendly than coal? Strangely enough, coal is allowed to be taken on the plane. The extraction of gas is getting increasingly difficult in any case; more recently, so-called utility companies have even come up with the idea of extracting shale gas from protected areas using questionable technologies.

Flying is an old dream of mankind, and the fear of crashing is a common human trauma. In the aircraft cabin, the risk of crashing is immediate, but the crashing of Spaceship Earth is an abstract and unimaginable thing. Crashed aircraft we know from the news; crashed worlds, we have not yet seen.

M920T
Supplied for British Airways by RR Donnelley

We read on in the fine print: liquid batteries are prohibited and we can only take batteries for our technological equipment in very small, harmless amounts. We have been so happy to master the future with e-mobility, and now that we've come to it, it's too dangerous. If the rules on the boarding pass would apply to Spaceship Earth, we might be able to feel as safe and comfortable on Earth as the airlines promise us for the duration of our flight. We would simply have to stick to the international baggage rules.

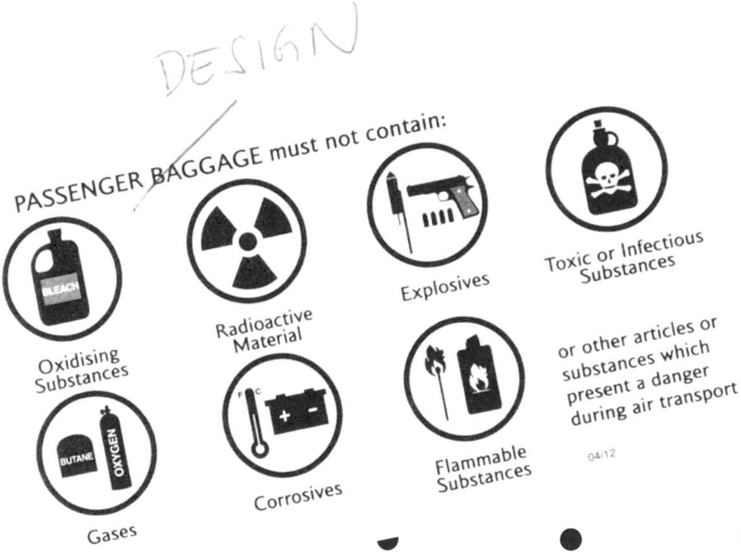

PASSENGER BAGGAGE must not contain:

DESIGN

- Oxidising Substances
- Gases
- Radioactive Material
- Corrosives
- Explosives
- Flammable Substances
- Toxic or Infectious Substances
- or other articles or substances which present a danger during air transport

The hand luggage metaphor also has a personal, philosophical dimension when we read how we should pack our luggage. One premier international airline advises us to decide in a "quiet moment" what we really need. Although this sounds stressful, as the quiet seems to last only for a moment, maybe we will see more clearly for that moment. Only the dimensions of the suitcase help us to restrict ourselves and to think about what is important (for this trip).

This is a revised version of the text "Handgepäck", published in: Friedrich von Borries, Jesko Fezer (eds.), 2013:216 ff.

Tools for the Design Revolution   19

(1.1) World Calculation Models

The mathematics of bag packing

We are perhaps the first generation that knows so precisely the extent of the destruction of the environment we have caused and the resulting dangerous effects on subsequent generations. We no longer have an excuse for uninformed action; future generations will be able to hold us accountable for it. The digital revolution makes it possible for a great deal of environmentally relevant information to be easy to understand, free and immediately accessible. Often the documents have names like "Summary for Decision Makers". In them, we find the latest numbers, as well as the trends for the next twenty, fifty or one hundred years. But who are the decision makers? Politicians? We should not rely on them, as the recent climate conferences have reached no decisions that stipulate a determined effort from the "decision makers" against global warming.

The worldwide struggle against poverty and global warming are among the most important challenges of our time and for subsequent generations. For that reason, these issues should also be at the top of the design agenda. But in the countries of the global North, design is the driving force of environmental degradation and social inequality. A lifestyle on a gigantic destructive scale has become the global model, and it threatens the future of the planet. A globally compatible lifestyle that is both affordable and desirable to all people should be our new goal – but what is "world-friendly"?

A world-friendly lifestyle
In its current fifth progress report, the Intergovernmental Panel on Climate Change (IPCC) has presented the scientific evidence for human-caused global warming so clearly as never before. Its chairman, Rajendra Kumar Pachauri, opened his lecture at the climate conference in Warsaw with a quote from Albert Einstein: "Problems cannot be solved at the same level of awareness that created them." In the future, we will need a new awareness of a type of design that is committed to sustainable lifestyles. One common definition of "sustainable design" is the balance of social, economic and environmental factors. Informed action should not be based on simplistic ideas and good intentions, but rather on facts.

The ecological footprint

In 1996, Mathis Wackernagel and William Rees published their book, *Our Ecological Footprint. Reducing Human Impact on the Earth*. The complex relationships that point to the resource consumption in our way of life imaginable, are represented by biocapacity and the ecological footprint. A world-friendly way of life naturally requires less or at most the same amount of available biocapacity. Today, however, we already consume 1.5 Earths per year (see diagram: footprint network), and if we continue like this, it will soon reach 3 Earths. The biocapacity of the Earth constantly decreases through overexploitation, and the world's population is increasing steadily. Thus, in the future, less and less biocapacity per capita will be available. There are also still many developing countries whose resource consumption is very low. According to current calculations, the available space for a world-friendly lifestyle would amount to about 1.8 global hectares per capita. This unit of measurement encompasses the average annual productivity of the world's biologically beneficial land and water areas. Developed countries already have a land use that is very far from this target, however, and have long been consuming several times their share of the available biocapacity.

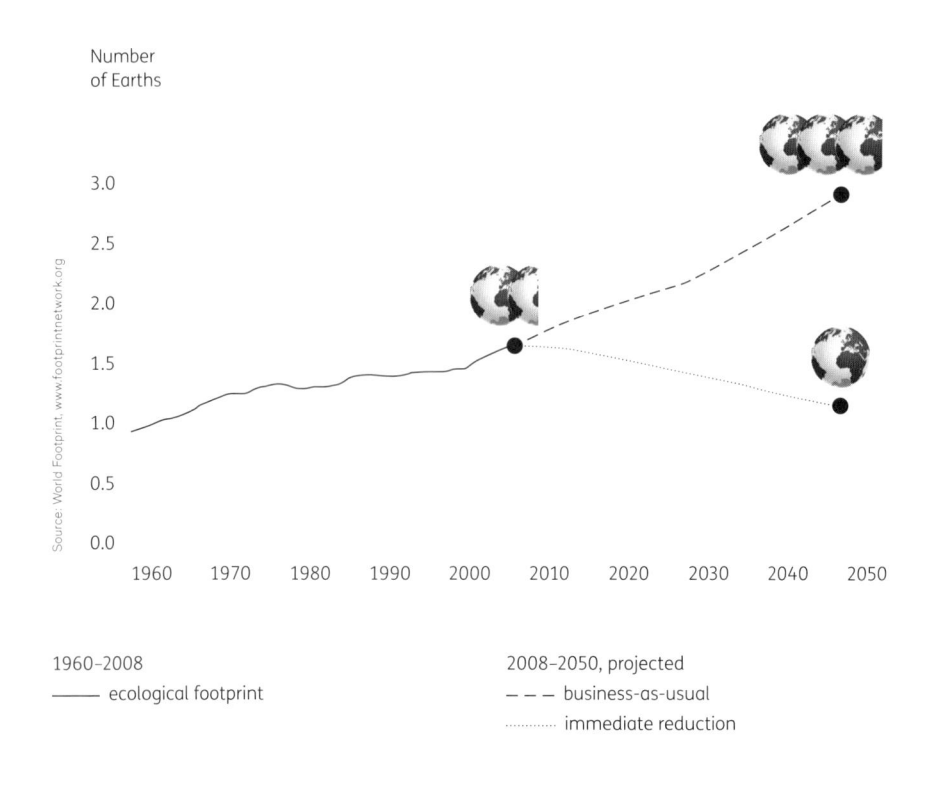

Number of Earths

Source: World Footprint, www.footprintnetwork.org

1960–2008
——— ecological footprint

2008–2050, projected
— — — business-as-usual
············ immediate reduction

22   Tools for the Design Revolution

One measure of Human Development
The ecological footprint is a good reference for the ecological component of our lifestyles. In addition, the Human Development Index (HDI) of the UNDP (United Nations Development Programme) summarizes the state of human development for all countries together on a scale from 0 to 1. Here, the life expectancy, education levels and purchasing power of a country's inhabitants are recorded. In the current *Human Development Report*, there is a diagram that links the ecological footprint of countries to their HDI – and here we see very clearly that countries with a high HDI unfortunately also have an environmentally destructive way of life. None of the countries with high living standards – and thus none of the so-called rich countries – have an environmentally friendly lifestyle!

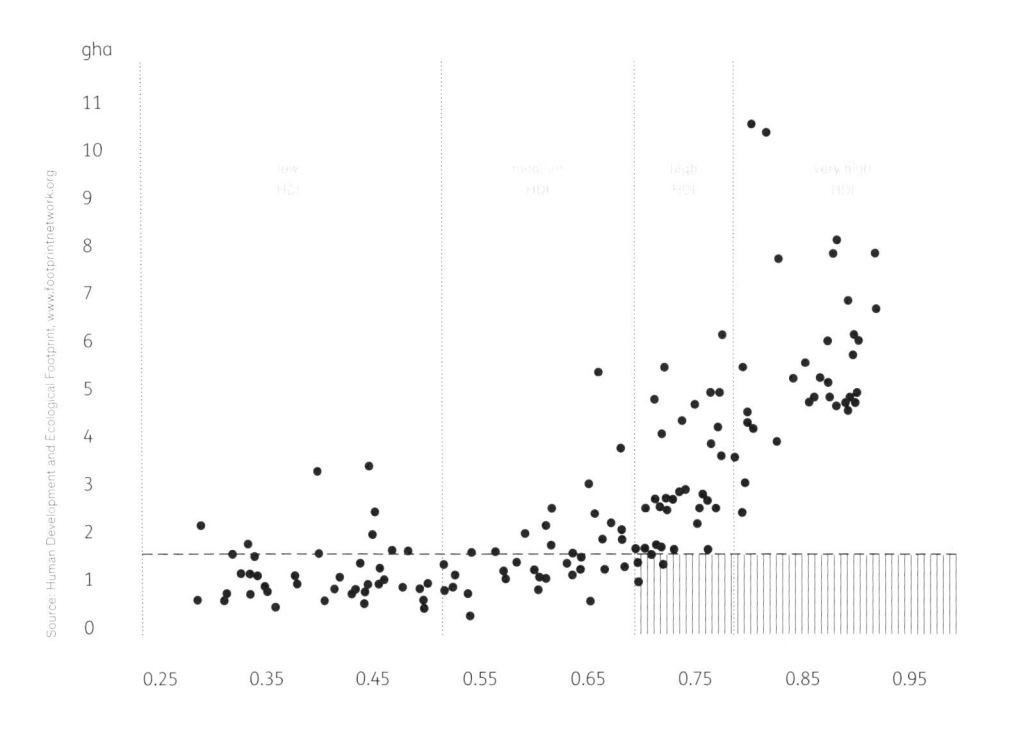

- country average per person
-- available biocapacity per person (1.8 gha)

||||||| sustainable human development

We can view the diagram as a strategic basis for the design revolution. On the homepage of the Global Footprint Network, the current ecological footprint of all countries can be looked up, and in the UNDP's report, the most recent HDI for each country can be found, giving its current position and offering a strategy for the future. Countries designated as highly developed must be placed on the path of sustainable development as soon as possible, and the countries designated as less developed should not necessarily imitate the mistakes of the developed countries.

(+) The ecological footprint is the currency of the future. Today, global finance is already verifying the impact of this factor on the currency markets. In 2011, the Global Footprint Network, together with the United Nations Environment Programme Finance Initiative (UNEP FI) and the major financial institutions, reviewed the relationship between environmental and financial risks for individual countries in a two-year project.

"The illusion that a high culture is one that uses the highest possible quantities of energy must be overcome if we are to get tools into focus. In classical societies power sources were very equally distributed."

Ivan Illich, 1973 (1998:48)

> "Limiting climate change will require substantial and sustained reductions of greenhouse gas emissions."
>
> IPCC, 2013:17

One ton of CO$_2$-eq

Very highly developed countries today have an average greenhouse gas emissions of 11.4 tons per capita per year (measured in CO$_2$ equivalents). Less developed countries emit around 0.4 tons, according to the UNDP. With a world-friendly lifestyle, one should be able to make due in the future with one ton of CO$_2$ equivalent! While the global South has yet to make the long and arduous journey to reach the formulated HDI, the so-called highly developed world must start on the path to a low-carbon society. One driver of high greenhouse gas emissions is humankind's energy consumption, since that energy is generated mainly by fossil fuels. Switzerland's 2,000-watt society initiative is committed to a sustainable and just society. Every person living now and in the future has a right to the same amount of energy!

The world formula
Approximately 2,000 watts of primary energy per person would be the measure of a solidarity-based, sustainable lifestyle. We would not be living in the Stone Age, because a life of prosperity and high quality for everyone is quite possible with this amount of energy. In the future, however, the proportion of fossil fuels would have to be drastically reduced. But at the moment, the world's population cannot even make that decision, due to the low prices of fossil fuel sources. We have updated the world formula according to current data from the International Energy Agency (IEA 2013:28) and the UN's statistics for the world's population. The amount of primary energy consumed today is divided by the number of people in the world, yielding approximately 2,000 watts per person.

(+) The world formula can be calculated with any globally available key resource shared by the world's population and time.

$$12{,}787{,}615{,}7...$$
$$\div\ 7{,}162{,}119{,}0...$$
$$=\ 1{,}785\ \text{watt}\ /$$

(+) In 2008, the city of Zurich committed itself to the goal of a 2,000-watt society. The citizens were informed about the objectives and are working together to try to come from their current level of 5,000 watts down to 2,000 watts, and to reduce CO_2 emissions by 80 percent from the current 5.5 tons per person per year to a maximum of one ton. In 2012, the city of Zurich for the first time measured its status on the way to a 2,000-watt society and determined that the consumption of primary energy has dropped from over 5,000 watts to approximately 4,200 watts per person between 1990 and 2012. So there is still a long way to go.

,741 watt
0 people

erson

2050

The city of Zurich's method for achieving the goal of one ton of CO_2-eq by 2050 could be called "proactive solidarity". No one is forcing us to do it – at least not yet. The path to a low-carbon society is a great opportunity for society, but also a challenge for the design of the future. A fundamentally new lifestyle must be developed, making it necessary to reconsider and reshape all of the elements of modern life. The next three to four decades are considered to be a realistic timeframe for implementing this new lifestyle – a period of time that many of us can still actively shape: not only through conscious design decisions, but also through consumer decisions and active political participation.

From the world to the individual

But what does that mean for the practice of design? How can these findings be applied to specific design tasks? How can you cut CO_2-eq by eighty to ninety percent? Our approach to transferring the global limits into everyday life involves the analysis of existing lifestyles. Today, the limits formulated above are the background for many different online calculators that can calculate the footprint of a person using algorithms of varying precision. Environmental organizations and national environmental ministries alike offer similar self-analytical tools that are simple and suitable for everyday use. Most of them also show the average value of the footprint for our own cultures – which, as we already know, is dramatically too high in the developed countries.

The One Tonne Life Project

In Sweden in 2011, under the academic supervision of the University of Chalmers, a family of four was catapulted into the future. A house from the 1970s, two old cars and summer holidays in Greece by plane formed the starting point for the project: a footprint of 7.3 tons of CO_2-eq per family member. Added to this is the "gray" footprint, which is calculated for Sweden at 1.8 tons of CO_2-eq. This makes 9.1 tons of CO_2-eq – quite far from one ton.

The ecological footprint was not tested in this experiment. We calculated it using a current footprint calculator: for the Swedish family, it would be a total of 8.18 gha. If all people were to live in this way, we would need almost five planets! Not a very world-friendly lifestyle. The gray energy – i.e., the amount of energy incurred by infrastructure and distributed to every citizen – would total 1.5 gha in this calculation.

For the family in the experiment, the largest contributor to their footprint in both analyses is their mobility. Two old cars and the summer air travel, as along with other mobility behavior, add up to three tons of CO_2-eq or 2.53 gha. Their diet has the second highest environmental impact: their high meat consumption and frequent eating in restaurants clocks in at 2.3 tons of CO_2-eq or 1.62 gha. The family's general consumption causes an additional ecological footprint of 1.2 tons of CO_2-eq or 1.24 gha. And with their old house, the housing area is another important environmental factor.

The graphical representation illustrates the differences between the ecological footprint and the CO_2-eq in the areas of food and housing. Nevertheless, the challenges are easy to identify – and at a minimum cost.

Ecological footprint in the "One Tonne Life" project, per person, annually (calculated by the IDRV)

gha

9
8.5
8
7.5
7
6.5
6
5.5
5
4.5
4
3.5
3
2.5
2
1.5
1
0.5
0

– – biocapacity per person annually

CO₂ emissions in the "One Tonne Life" project, per person, annually (calculated by One Tonne Life)

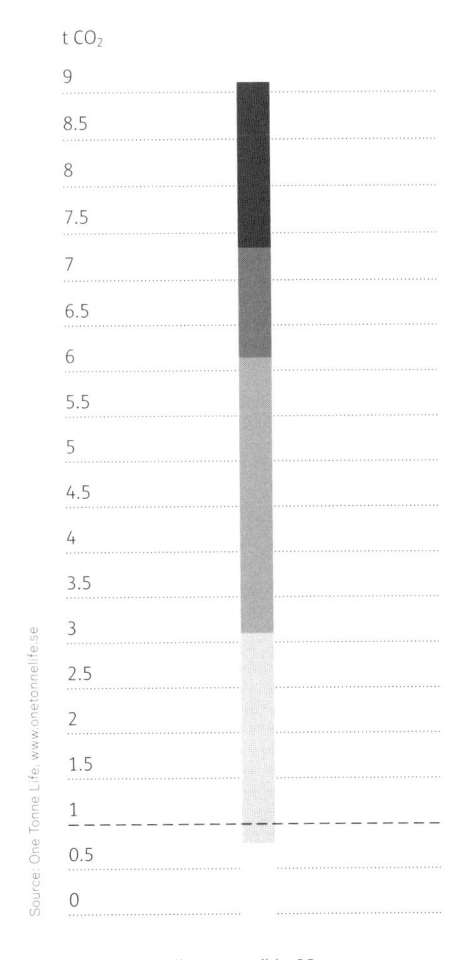

t CO₂

9
8.5
8
7.5
7
6.5
6
5.5
5
4.5
4
3.5
3
2.5
2
1.5
1
0.5
0

Source: One Tonne Life, www.onetonnelife.se

– – environmentally compatible CO₂ emissions per person per year (IPCC)

■ housing   ▒ nutrition   ■ mobility   ■ consumption   ■ gray footprint (public consumption)

Tools for the Design Revolution   29

Life in the future

How can the family in the experiment, currently at such a high output level, come even into the vicinity of a sustainable lifestyle? Swedish industry sponsored a passive house, an electric car and green electricity. Is that enough? Is the assertion of industry that we only need to buy the "right" things correct? The family moved into the new house and was pleased with the electric car. But after a few weeks it was clear that without a dramatic change of lifestyle, the purchasable ecology fetishes of industry would not be of much help. The only solution is no long distance travel, less meat and less driving. We have known this for a long time, but it actually applies to the family in the experiment as well. With a little good will and the sponsorship of industry, CO_2-eq was reduced by fifty percent – still far from the required one ton. After that, measures that are far less bearable for our way of life came into use: vegan diet, no eating out, short showers, no traveling, second-hand clothes. Not counting the gray footprint, our future travelers actually reached 1.5 tons for a short time. The Swedish Environment Minister redeemed the family by ceremonially shutting off the house's on-board computer after six months: minus 79 percent.

The aforementioned example can be easily understood with any footprint calculator. In this way, you can get a feel for the impact of your lifestyle. In our calculation, the family's ecological footprint would have decreased by a total of 68.5 percent, reaching a lifestyle that – if the entire world population lived this way – would consume only 1.5 Earths. "Congratulations! You already have a future-proof lifestyle. Share your experience about this 'good life with a small footprint' with as many people as possible," the digital life consultant praises us for our factitious lifestyle. Over ninety percent savings in housing and mobility, a maximum of 83 percent in the diet, and modest consumption reduces the footprint by sixty percent. Although the original lifestyle of the family does not seem particularly exaggerated, it was still greatly enhanced at 154 percent of the average lifestyle. The radically reduced lifestyle is about 54 percent of the average, and in the future, the gray footprint will hopefully go down as well. Therefore we need a collective effort to crucially improve the environmental impact of our infrastructure.

(+) The use of footprint calculators is free and easy. The calculations give an initial reference point for effective design interventions. Objectives can be defined and various measures to achieve them can be tried.

(+) The consideration of lifestyles plays a more important role than the isolated consideration of products or services.

Reduction of the ecological footprint in the "One Tonne Life" project, per person, annually (calculated by the IDRV)

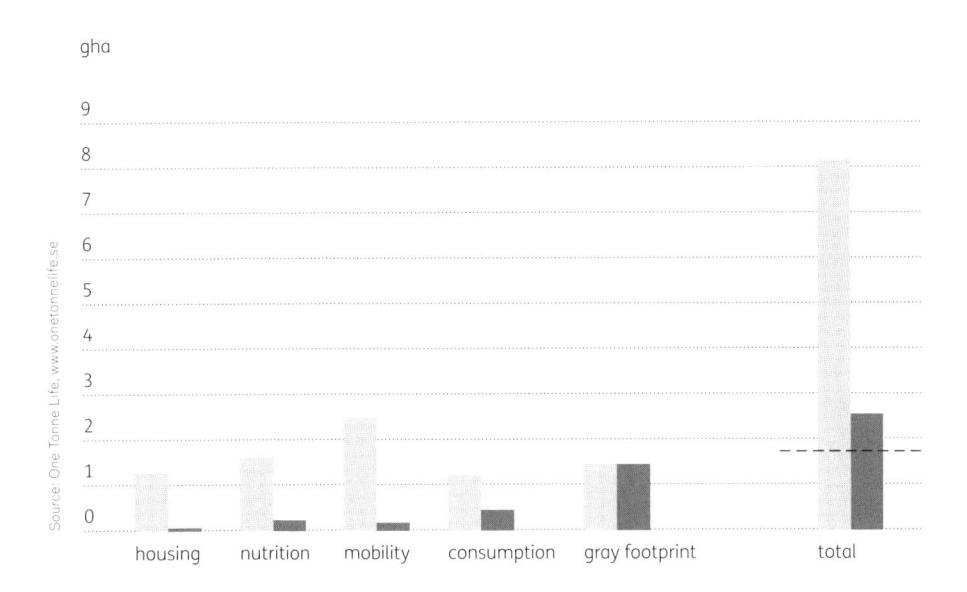

gha

Source: One Tonne Life, www.onetonnelife.se

Bar chart showing values for housing, nutrition, mobility, consumption, gray footprint, and total, comparing values at the beginning of the project versus after lifestyle adjustments.

-- biocapacity per person annually

▫ at the beginning of the project
▪ after lifestyle adjustments

Tools for the Design Revolution   31

2

Tools for the Design Revolution

Tools for the Design Revolution

❷ Stimulants

"The whole community, in fact, was cast into the jaws of this ravening monster, 'the cheap production' forced upon it by the World-Market."

William Morris, 1891 (1991:103)

The design revolution is as old as the industrial revolution.

Design revolutionary
William Morris (1834–1896, England) was perhaps one of the first design revolutionaries. Pollution and the lack of both artistic and material quality in industrial production led to his preference for alternative, handcrafted production. Unfortunately, only the rich could afford the products created in this way. Morris was fascinated by the Middle Ages and from it, he developed motifs and stories for a fictional future. This can bee seen in particular in his novel, *News from Nowhere*, which catapults us into an ideal future world, with factories that emit no pollutants, a lifestyle like a holiday, and the best part: no money is needed, but excellent goods and services are still available. The inhabitants of *Nowhere* work according to their mood and whim. It is only too bad that the women were not yet emancipated.

The reality
His idea workshop in the real world was collectively organized as a cooperative enterprise, and thus as a progressive alternative to capitalist production conditions. William Morris had inherited his money, though cynics would say that was the only way he could afford to have his socialist ideas. That may be true, but he did not have to act on them; he could have just as easily put his capital into an exploitative factory. Human and material resources have been used since the beginning of the industrial revolution in ways that are not forward-looking. Even today, we hear about distant countries where our consumer goods are produced under conditions that would have shocked us a hundred years ago.

⚠ Morris criticized the problem of the world market at the beginning of the industrial revolution. In his science fiction novel, it has already collapsed, and society is once again characterized by local modes of production, creativity and self-determination.

⊕ In his book *Small is Beautiful* (1971), Ernst Friedrich Schumacher challenged the megalomania and globalization fantasies of his time with the slogan "small is beautiful". He called for a technological revolution to produce methods and equipment that are affordable and accessible to everyone, are applicable on a small scale and that meet the human need for creativity.

"Society can be destroyed when further growth of mass production renders the milieu hostile, when it extinguishes the free use of the natural abilities of society's members, when it isolates people from each other and locks them into a man-made shell, when it undermines the texture of community by promoting extreme social polarization and splintering specialization, or when cancerous acceleration enforces social change at a rate that rules out legal, cultural, and political precedents as formal guidelines to present behavior."

Ivan Illich, 1973 (1998:11)

Critique of growth

In the early 1970s, the philosopher Ivan Illich (1926–2002) was invited by the Prime Minister of Canada to express the characteristic, epoch-specific bias of his time. His answer was growth – and the uncritical faith in the positive connection between institutional value and fairness or justice. For Illich, the crisis of the industrial mode of production will either lead to its own downfall by machinery, or to a way out in which the people opt for what he calls "convivial tools".

Tools for conviviality

Illich wanted people to escape from the hamster wheel of industrial productivity. He longed for a change brought about by the fact that people have not only lost their faith in paper currency, but also in industrial productivity. This would lead to transformation of society and the prevailing system of production, which would empower autonomous individuals and primary groups to participate in the system of production in an alternative way. "Conviviality" is the opposite of industrial productivity. Convivial tools give the people who use them the best possible opportunity to enrich the environment with the results of their visions. They create a society in which individuals, not managers, make use of modern technologies. Progress, which has made us socially dependent, is therefore replaced by a notion of progress that is synonymous with an improvement in the people's ability to help themselves.

Self-limitation

Ivan Illich's concept of conviviality could also characterize the study *Prosperity without Growth: Economics for a Finite Planet* (2009) by the economist Tim Jackson. Jackson calls for a change in the economy and in society: a transformation of the economy into an ecologically conscious macroeconomics, and a change in society into a sphere where, unlike today, participation in social life is possible even without consumption. He sees prosperity as threatened not by recession, but by an endlessly growing materialism, which is inscribed for the future of the economic model practiced today. The measures that Jackson proposes include establishing limits, repairing the economic model and altering the logic of society. Hopefully the time will soon be ripe for this change!

(+) In his account *Walden; or, Life in the Woods* (1854), Henry David Thoreau (1817–1862) made an early attempt at a self-determined, alternative lifestyle. He radically redefined his life necessities by moving to a self-built log cabin on Walden Pond. What do you really need?

Transition Towns

A movement that seeks to free cities from their dependence on oil and establish new forms of production based on self-determination, especially in agriculture (permaculture, community gardens). The use of local currencies helps to grant additional independence. Rob Hopkins, the movement's founder, has written *The Transition Handbook* (2008), a guide to transforming today's cities into "Transition Towns". At the same time, however, we must not be lured into a medieval romance.

New Work

A movement, initiated by social philosopher Frithjof Bergmann (b. 1930), which propagates a new division of labor. In his book *Neue Arbeit, neue Kultur* (New Work, New Culture, 2004), Bergmann advocates reducing gainful employment to one third. Thus freed, one third of the workday would be used in the future for producing people's own goods using new technologies. Simple design would make it possible for people to produce their own goods – even complex goods such as houses or cars, locally in the future – and, thanks to this high-tech in-house production, to be independent from global consumption. Another third of the workday would be used for the things that you "really, really" want to do. This personal development of the individual results in added value for society, whose aim is self-determined work.

"To make the world work for 100% of humanity in the shortest possible time through spontaneous cooperation without ecological offense or the disadvantage of anyone."

R. Buckminster Fuller (2008:inside cover)

Open design

Ivan Illich called the systems and institutions that are dominated by individuals "destructive tools". The proliferation of independent, technologically well-equipped manufacturing workshops (FabLabs) is already the beginning of a new logic of production. In this context, a culture of design has emerged that is characterized by new collaborations and often also by the free availability of digital construction plans (copyleft instead of copyright). In the future, a direct relationship will form between users and designers. A clearly differentiated and self-determined formulation of the legal claims of creatives (Creative Commons) governs the sharing of design (re-use, adaptation and use) in ways that go beyond the capitalist logic of production and exploitation.

A new world

One protagonist for the design of the future is R. Buckminster Fuller (1895–1983). He was an architect, engineer, geometrician, cartographer, philosopher, futurist, inventor and author of nearly thirty books. He designed a new world with technological houses (Dymaxion House) that were radically dematerialized and were suspended almost weightlessly by a central column. He dreamed of a new generation of cars (Dymaxion Car) and also discovered a new cartographic representation of the whole world (Dymaxion World). The map lays there as if shattered to pieces, and can be arranged on the plane in different ways to tell geopolitical stories. On a large scale, his geodesic domes were also dematerialized structures that emerged from his mathematical research and could perhaps even cover entire neighborhoods.

The World Game

Buckminster Fuller conceived of a dome for the U.S. contribution to the 1967 World Expo in Montreal. Since the 1950s, he was occupied by the looming social and environmental crisis. In order to finally open people's eyes to the problem, he designed the "World Game", which should be played until all the people in the world have sufficient resources for their lives without destroying the planet further. Each game decision should be visualized by a computer so that the global impact of the decision is obvious.

The game board was the Dymaxion World. Over the years, Buckminster Fuller collected data on the world's resources. In a research project from 1965 to 1975 (the World Design Science Decade), architecture schools around the world were to consider how not just forty percent (1961) but one hundred percent of the population could utilize the world's resources.

Spaceship Earth

Buckminster Fuller's book *Operating Manual for Spaceship Earth* (1969) presents us with the Earth as a spaceship, with us humans as astronauts on board. But our spaceship does not come with instructions. In critical situations like today, we have to get by without a manual. The fossil fuel reserves on our spaceship have been greatly depleted over a few generations and should be urgently converted to renewable energy sources. A revolution in efficiency would be necessary to ensure that the world's resources can supply the entire world's population. Perhaps an automatic control might solve the problem and still allow a happy landing for all of humanity? Fuller's appeal is just as relevant now as then:

> "So, planners, architects, and engineers take the initiative. Go to work, and above all co-operate and don't hold back on one another and try to gain on the expense of another."

R. Buckminster Fuller, 1969 (2008:138)

3

+ 548.36 L water

Tools for the Design Revolution 43

③ Recipes

1 Kilogram of pasta – made with: 100% durum wheat semolina

Ingredients

13.1 g	gravel/sand
8.6 g	potassium
6.6 g	phosphorus
5.1 g	lime
1.7 g	alogenate
2.8 g	others

Energy

86.4 g	coal
148.2 g	oil
136.4 g	natural gas
<0.1 g	uranium
0.1 g	others
138.7 L	water

44   Tools for the Design Revolution

To make one kilogram of pasta that meets the claim on the package of 100 percent durum wheat semolina, first cultivate a wheat field, fertilize it with 6.6 g of phosphorus, and mix in 0.6 g of sand, 8.5 g of potassium, 2.5 g of lime, 1.7 g of alogenate and 0.2 g of other materials. Water it with 133.4 liters of water. Consume energy in the form of 20 g of coal, 70.8 g of oil and 32.7 g of gas. If nuclear energy is produced in your country, add trace amounts (<0.1 g) of uranium. Now bring the gathered wheat to the mill and add 0.2 g of lime and 0.3 liters of water, and in the milling process use an additional 10.7 g of coal, 15.2 g of oil and 9.4 g of gas (and possibly some small amounts of uranium). To process the newly created durum wheat semolina into pasta, add 2 g of sand, 1.6 g of lime, 1.4 g of other materials and 2.9 L of water, and form this into pasta using energy from 39 g of coal, 4.4 g of oil, 65.8 g of gas and possibly some uranium.

Don't forget to bag and package the corn and the pasta; for this, you need 10.5 g of sand, 0.1 g of potassium, 0.7 g of lime and 1.2 g of other materials, plus energy in the amount of 11.9 g of coal, 5.6 g of oil, 25.5 g of gas and maybe some uranium. To transport your pasta, you need an additional 0.1 g of lime and energy in the form of 4.8 g of coal, 52.2 g of oil, 3 g of gas and some uranium. Now you are almost done: place the pasta in a pot of water and boil using additional energy until it suits your taste.

The discrepancies between "contents" and content

This data refers to a world average in pasta production and varies by country.
The pasta example shows that the ingredient list on the package for 100% durum wheat semolina represents only a fraction of the true ingredients, so to speak. Only a look at the Environmental Product Declaration (EPD) on the pasta manufacturer's website reveals all of the ingredients required to produce that one kilogram of pasta made from durum wheat semolina. In order to calculate the ecological footprint for the production of pasta, we must count not just the water for cooking, but also what was used in the production phase: the phosphorus that was scattered on the wheat fields in the form of fertilizer, and the energy that, depending on the country of production, was obtained from a different mix of various fossil fuels and possibly even dangerous fuel sources.

The Consequences
of De

Köln
International
School
of Design

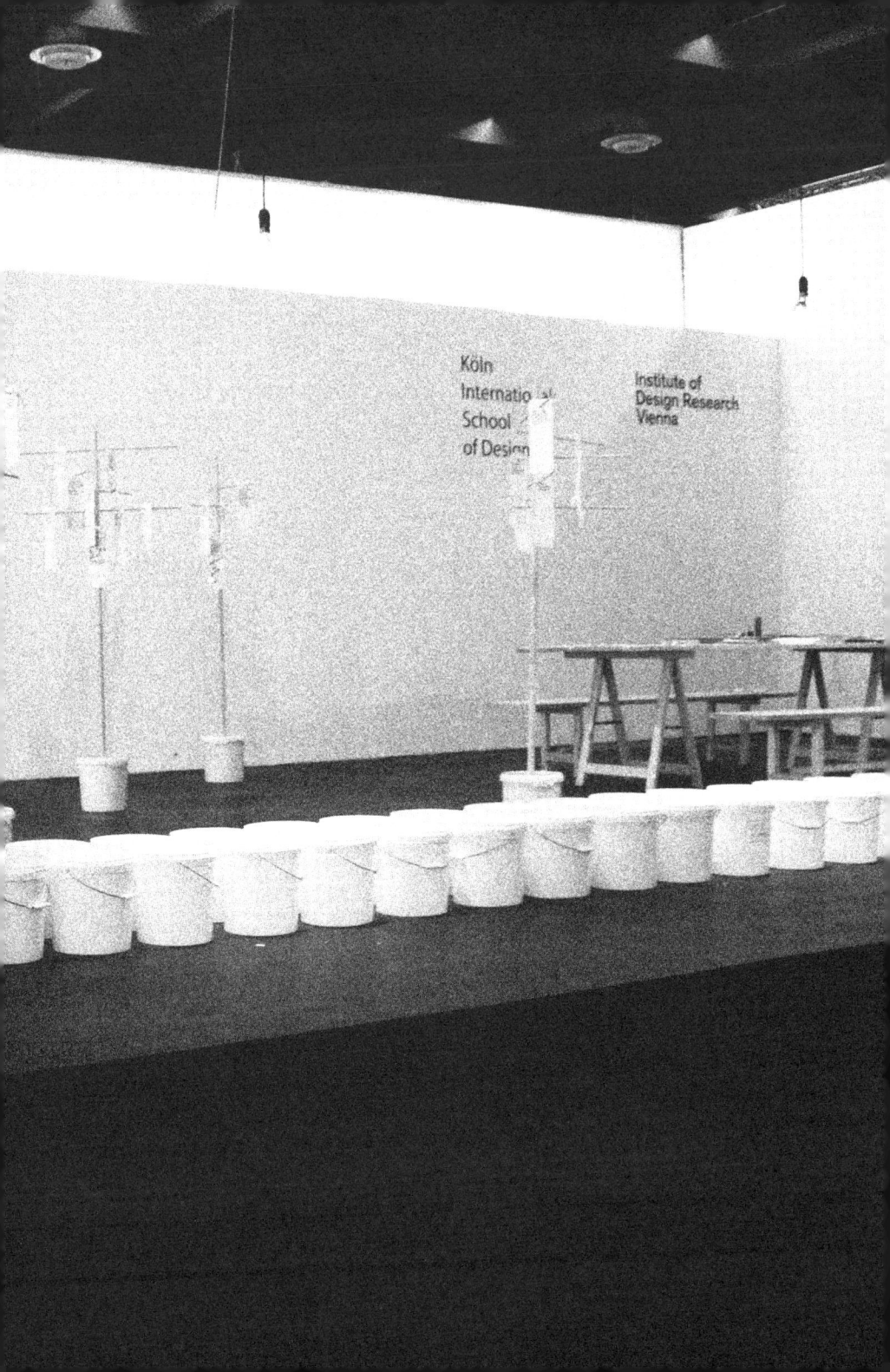

Institute of
Design Research
Vienna

1 Plastic stacking chair with four metal legs

Ingredients

1.45 g	iron
0.11 g	salt
0.76 g	lime
0.72 g	gravel/sand
0.09 g	nickel
0.08 g	chromium
0.12 g	others
3.83 g	coal
3.53 g	oil
2.49 g	natural gas
0.81 g	biomass
548.36 L	water

see pages 42/43

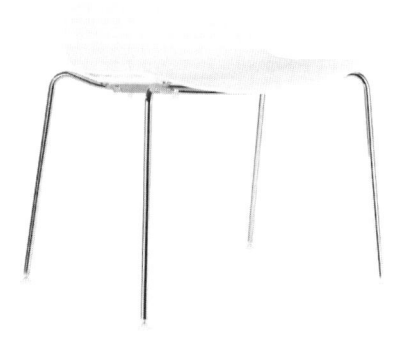

For a plastic stacking chair with a metal frame, not only is 2.6 liters of crude oil needed to produce the plastic, but also a small amount of crude oil is also proportionally used in the processing of raw materials, manufacturing, packaging and transportation. The environmental product declaration gives a 15-year product life cycle, and in these 15 years, 22.7 liters of water will be needed to clean the chair. This represents about 4% of the total water needs – the amount of water that accrues over the entire life of the chair. So after producing the chair and 15 years of use, we are sitting on nearly 550 liters of water. Moreover, the small amounts of chromium, nickel and calcium, depending on the composition, are by no means harmless. According to the warnings on the packaging of these chemical elements, if even trace amounts should enter through the respiratory tract, they can cause health problems.

Dealing with recipes

Products are obviously made out of the materials that we perceive with our senses in the moment when we handle and use them. The components we perceive are not always harvested directly from trees or extracted from the ground, however. They are the result of various processes that, in turn, require other raw materials, which have their own energy requirements that should not be underestimated. While we may be curious about the ingredients in delicacies and in good cooking and baking recipes, and inquire about their preparation, the composition of products remains a secret. In the context of EU directives, manufacturers are increasingly being asked to disclose their ingredients in environmental product declarations (EPDs) and break them down according to product life cycles. While some manufacturers provide this data voluntarily, others advertise their company's use of life cycle assessments, but only reveal percentage-based information about improvements per life cycle.

⚠ It makes sense, as a consumer and a designer, to insist on having access to EPDs, which are the most internationally standardized and transparent tool available. If this content information is not present, you can confront the respective manufacturers and ask for it.

But EPDs alone are not enough. The recipes contain no information about the exact origin of the raw materials and the social conditions under which they were extracted. Commodity prices, too, are not indicative of the fair remuneration of the workers in the mines and the fields. A large proportion of the commodity price is artificially generated on stock exchanges, and benefits only the speculators, so a precise breakdown of costs and origin is necessary. Even the manufacturers do not always have this information. Multi-part supply chains should therefore be even more transparent in the future, and commodities should only be purchased if this information is made available unsolicited and comprehensibly.

⚠ As a designer, I can ask for the exact product information and draw attention to any abuses in order to increase the pressure on those responsible.

The relationship between use and ownership

Only by representing the ingredients can we see the amount of resources required for our products. Many of them are things we want to own unconditionally, and then store them in our cabinets and drawers to use only two or three times a year. If we were to inventory our lives and our environment and calculate exactly what has been purchased by an average household – for example, in Germany – the result would be the mountain of resources listed on the right, which shows that we do not live with a very small footprint. It is important to know the large and small impacts of our actions in order to understand the need for a less resource-intensive lifestyle.

An average human life in Germany

245 t	sand and gravel
215 t	hard stones
170 t	lignite
105 t	mineral oil
95	natural gas (in 1,000 m^3)
70 t	limestone, dolomite
65 t	coal
40 t	steel
27 t	cement
14 t	rock salt
12 t	clay
9 t	quartz
7 t	gypsum, anhydrite
4 t	kaolinite
3 t	aluminum
3 t	copper
2 t	peat
0.7 t	bentonite
0.7 t	zinc
0.6 t	potash (K$_2$O)
0.5 t	sulfur
0.4 t	lead
0.4 t	feldspar
0.4 t	fluorite
0.3 t	barite
0.1 t	phosphate

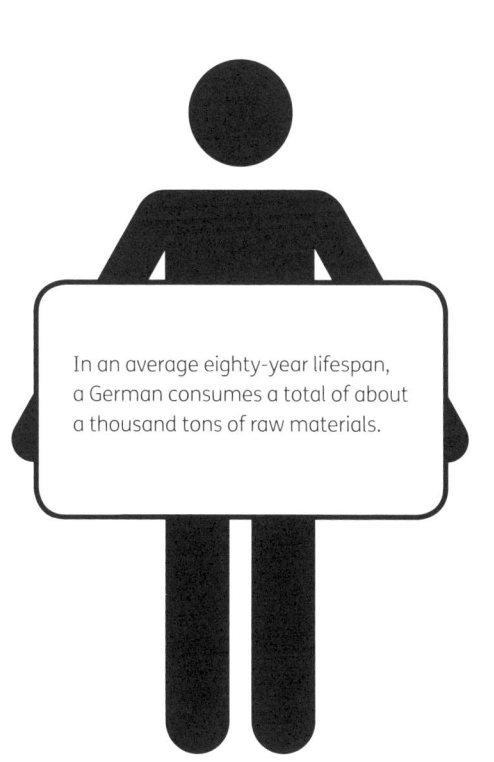

Source: German Federal Institute for Geosciences and Natural Resources, 2008

In an average eighty-year lifespan, a German consumes a total of about a thousand tons of raw materials.

4

gaga di bling blong
gaga blung

table one: lifecycledada	systemboundary	sssyyysssteeemmm-booooouuuundary
eu-twentyseven	norm norm norm DIN	•••• one two three thousand
	one two three	hundred thousand
	99 g cee oh two/km (combined)	•••• numbers numbers numbers n-u-m-b-e-r-s
table two dark red slash	purple red slash	light red slash
first long	second half-long	third eighth-long
	Environmental profile ••••	Environmental impact ••••
	Environmental rating ••••	Environmental footprint ••••
table three	CEE OH TWO.	EN OH EX
	ess oh two	cee aych four
	EN EM VEE OH CEE	primaryenergyconsumption
onehundredten kilograms	thirtythreepointfive kilograms	andsoforth
systemboundary	4.6/3.3/3.8 L/100km	(city/highway/combined)

52 Tools for the Design Revolution

table four
dark yellow slash   yellow slash   lemon yellow slash

first short   second half-long   third long

70/220/EEC   arrow

table five   one two three four five

ten cee oh two   eleven cee oh two   twelve cee oh two

fourpointfive   zeropointtwoseven-
sevenone

1 kilogram cee oh two   0.502 kilograms cee oh two

presentation of analysis   arrow   worst case?

table six
dark-blue slash   light-blue slash   green-blue slash

inverse relationship

Eleven One

everything is in the green   Environmental Rating:
valuable

gadji beri bimba   glandridi laula lonni   cadori

BILANZDADA
an onomatopoeic interpretation of the life cycle analysis
inspired by *gadji beri bimba*,
sound poem by Hugo Ball, 1916

Tools for the Design Revolution   53

④ Life Cycle Analysis

Out with the white coats! Designing a life cycle

⚠ Designing the entire life cycle of a product or service requires situation-dependent design decisions.

Each one has direct and indirect consequences on the environment and on people that are not obvious at first, and their global dimension is too complex to make such decisions on a gut level.

Who can easily estimate the impact that the raw material extraction process will have on the environment, and then compare this with the life cycle scenario of a product? It is irresponsible to decide on a gut level which material is better, ecologically speaking, for a bicycle frame, for example. There are material libraries for testing the visual and tactile qualities of materials, books on their technical properties – which are even understandable by non-engineers – as well as estimates of the costs of sourcing and processing. Ways to make informed decisions are already in place, but one criterion that has been neglected is the environmental and social impact of these very decisions. Here we cannot yet rely on experience. And were we to ask the question of whether aluminum or steel would be a better alternative, we could fill long pro-and-con lists for both materials and still answer the question only with ifs and buts. As the "Recipes" chapter shows, we are not always aware of the variety of resources that are used in the manufacturing of products. As in a cost projection, a life cycle analysis lists a product's expenditure items, multiplies them by the impact factors and then finally adds in the respective effects. The results of a life cycle analysis can be processed by independent organizations as part of an environmental product declaration (EPD) for a product or a service.

A life cycle assessment represents and evaluates the effects a product or system can have on the environment and on people in its various phases. This makes it possible to find the effective levers or hot spots in relation to sustainable products and systems, and to make informed design decisions. Ideally, they give us information about the environmental impact from the extraction of raw materials, their processing, the distribution of the finished product and its use, up to an end-of-life scenario – that is, over the entire life cycle. Therefore, a life cycle assessment is a prerequisite for thinking in terms of material flows. But what happens with the product at the end of its life cycle must be determined realistically in a life cycle assessment.

Six steps to a life cycle assessment

1. At the beginning of a life cycle assessment, the objectives and requirements for the evaluation of the products or services under evaluation must be defined. LCAs allow the indicated and important targets from the world computation models to be examined. They also allow two or more products to be compared to one another, or a new or further development in an old product to be evaluated, or only the changes in the individual stages of the life cycle to be examined.

For the chair example from the "Recipes" chapter, that can mean comparing the existing chair and a design in the new product language of the manufacturer with the existing life cycle analysis. The new design should receive an environmental certificate in order to be used in public buildings.

2. In a second step, a functional unit or a service unit must be found. This corresponds to the system requirement of the methods/products under examination. By adopting a consumption or functional usage unit, a breadth of alternatives in the usage phase can be compared.

The chair's functional unit is to serve as a seat for 15 years.

(+) The goal of the design tasks for the future is no longer to design a product, but a functional unit, a benefit or a service.

This leads to alternatives and allows a view of the bigger picture that breaks the dictates of industry – merely to design this product – and creates a new culture, and with it a new concept of innovation.

3. Next, a scenario for the entire life cycle must be created. What raw materials are needed? How will they be processed? How does the product get to the user? What is the purpose of the product? Under what conditions and how long will it be used on average? What happens during recycling? Are the resources destroyed ("cradle to grave") or transferred in a cycle ("cradle to cradle")?

The chair has four steel legs and a seat shell made of plastic (PP); it is manufactured in a factory that sources the plastic and the steel each from local suppliers. The finished chairs are sold through dealers across Europe. The frame and the seat shells are individually packaged in a carton. After 15 years, the product will be replaced and disposed of. Only disposal in the country of manufacture is considered here.

⚠ It is important to consider different scenarios. Local production, varying transport routes for the materials, types of packaging and durability can have a significant impact on the overall balance. Define your system boundaries so that you have a comparable and manageable framework for your scenarios. What influencing factors do you include, and what do you exclude? The system boundaries have to be set so that they exclude areas that are not relevant to the life cycle assessment and correspond to realistic scenarios.

For some product categories, EPDs (Environmental Product Declarations) can already be found. There, the scenarios and system boundaries are defined at the outset. Try to orient yourself according to these documents. For certain products, the usage scenarios are defined for the LCA and found in the product category rules (PCRs).

For the chair, the PCRs for the environmental certification of group seating presumes that they will end up in the garbage after 15 years of use.

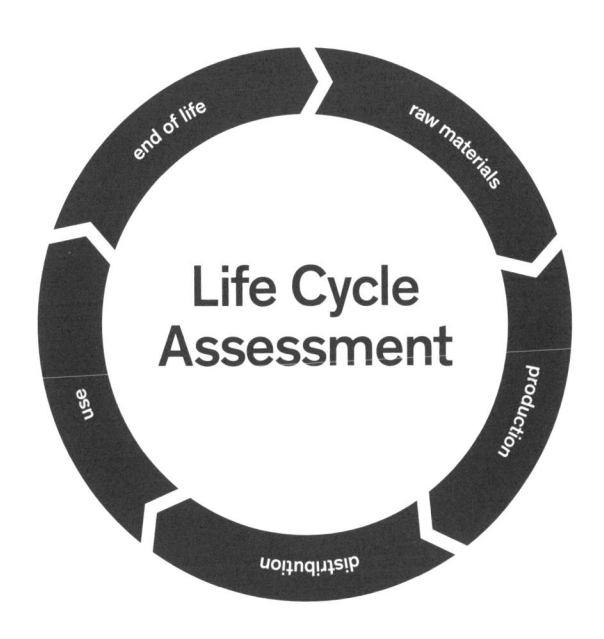

Life Cycle Assessment

- raw materials
- production
- distribution
- use
- end of life

Tools for the Design Revolution

4. Representing the material flow.
A detailed analysis of the required resources – known in the literature as a life cycle inventory (LCI) – is part of an LCA and represents the material flow necessary for a product system. It includes the amounts of water, energy and raw materials that are required.

Mapping the material flow ensures that, in addition to the raw materials, the necessary energy requirements for their exploitation and a comprehensive number of other secondary materials are also included on the balance sheet. During the manufacture of a product, and in all the various project and production phases, energy and other resources are needed, each of which might bring their own chain of required resources.

For this very detailed presentation, there is LCA software which already includes material chains.

To create the list of ingredients for a chair: Supplier 1 needs crude oil and other materials for the production of PP, while supplier 2 needs iron. Both consume energy and water. The materials are brought to the factory by truck, meaning that fuel – i.e., crude oil – is consumed. In the factory, the materials are processed and refined, where materials, water and energy are again consumed. In the country of manufacture, electricity is derived in part from coal, gas, uranium, etc.

**Abstract representation
of material flows**

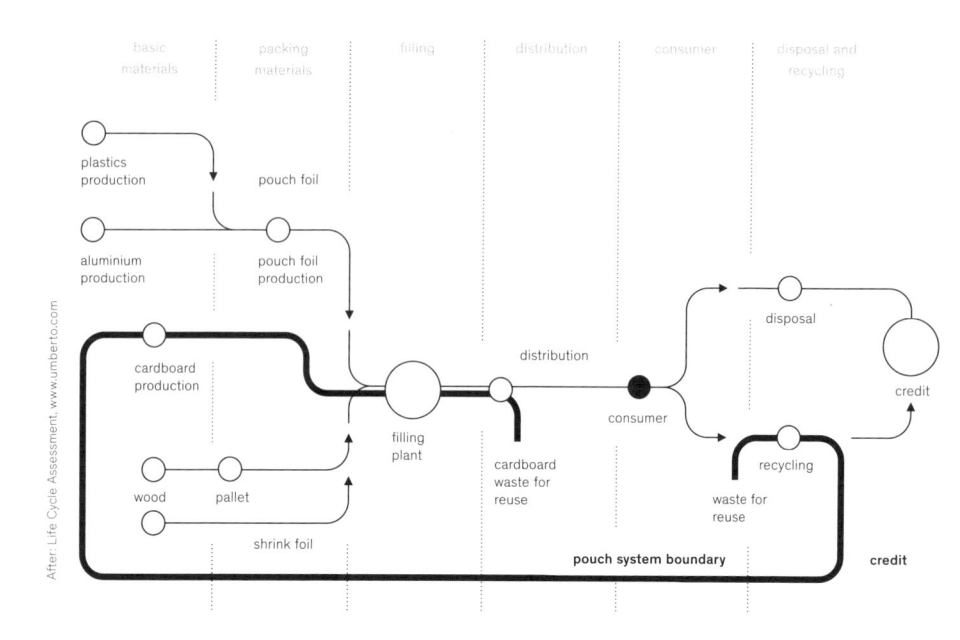

⚠ A simple representation of the material flow can be created on a sheet of paper or in a spreadsheet and gives an overview of the variety and quantity of resources needed for different components. A plastic part, for example, consists of plastic granules, which require, among other things, crude oil, energy and water. The granules are injection-molded using energy.

⚠ Manufacturers and suppliers should be able to provide this information. It is normally documented in the managerial software. If the data is not there, energy and water consumption can be measured.
All of the materials that go into the factory are contained proportionally in the products that leave the factory.

5. The necessary amounts must be quantified.

The chair manufacturer's suppliers can give their energy and water consumption proportionally to the required amounts of PP and iron by dividing the total consumption by the quantity of the material produced. They know what amounts of oil or iron ore they need. In the factory, electricity and water consumption can also be measured and divided by the number of chairs produced. The amounts needed for transport can be determined by the means of transport and the routes covered. The packaging material can be weighed. In the 15-year life of the chair, it will also be cleaned several times a year, for which you need a little water. The disposal facility also has certain power and water requirements and can specify this in proportion to the quantity to be disposed of.

6. Now the needed resources can be correlated with impact indicators and these factors can then be multiplied by the quantity of item 5 (LCIA – life cycle impact assessment). Every product, every process and every action has a direct and indirect impact on the environment, on people and on the available resources. A detailed LCA provides information on the impacts on the greenhouse effect, over-fertilization, ozone depletion, summer smog and acid rain. The indicators are stored in databases that are accessible only in part. Information and references can be found at the respective federal environmental agencies, however.

The chair manufacturer has commissioned an independent organization to prepare the environmental certificate. There, the determined values are typed into the LCA software and the effects on humans and the environment at each stage of the product life cycle and in total are spat out.

⚠ In each life cycle assessment, the effect to be analyzed and evaluated must be identified at the beginning. The selection of these influencing categories specifies the calculation methodologies to be used.

⚠ Impacts on the greenhouse effect, over-fertilization, ozone depletion, summer smog and acid rain always result. They cause indirect damage to the environment and to humans and affect the quality and availability of resources. Everyone needs to be aware of this relationship.

Postscript on the evaluation units
One feasible way is to create a product carbon footprint (PCF) or CO_2 footprint and to use information on CO_2 equivalents. The CO_2 footprint is an established method of environmental evaluation and can already be found for many products. It describes the balance of greenhouse gas emissions throughout the life cycle of a product or service in a defined scenario and refers to the functional unit. "Greenhouse gas emissions" refers to the total amount of gaseous substances that have been determined to have a coefficient for global warming potential (GWP) by the IPCC. The CO_2 footprint is therefore measured in units of CO_2-eq (carbon dioxide equivalent).

As the designer of a new chair, we can work in steps 1 through 5 and weigh the effects of different design decisions throughout the entire design process using a CO_2 balance. The CO_2-eq values for electricity are available for each country and at each electricity provider. The values for the materials can be found in the EPLCA Life Cycle Data Network or in commercial LCA databases, for example. Through the life cycle assessment, we recognize the potential for a better CO_2 footprint and can help shape this. For example, you can save 50 percent of the packaging material and volume by packing the seat shell and frame in a cardboard box.

⚠ As we know from our ingredients box, CO_2 is not the only relevant environmental factor. Often different materials are built into products that will sooner or later become scarce, or that cannot be adequately recycled with today's technologies. Also, the extraction of raw materials often happens under inhumane circumstances – or the environment is contaminated not through the air, but through the soil and the water. The effects of other pollutants are ignored and no details on the quality or the depletion of resources are given. The CO_2 footprint does not allow the assessment of a working recovered substance cycle. Nevertheless, CO_2 is an important limiting factor globally, as described in more detail in the chapter on the world formula.

⚠ Data on the CO_2-eq of resources can be found in databases, taken from life cycle assessment tools, or derived from existing CO_2 footprints and LCAs. For processes for which no data is available, values can be estimated, for example using values for similar manufacturing processes or for a similar material category. But ask manufacturers, suppliers and environmental experts first for the missing values!

⊕ This data should be freely available to all designers at any time, so please share the results and figures that are important for environmental assessments and exchange ideas with other experts and colleagues.

Postscript on life cycle assessment tools for designers

There are a number of tools targeted at designers that enable the evaluation of different decisions in the design process. They can initially be divided into "free to use" and "paid". In addition, they inform about different impact categories. Some tools function with cumulative values/indicators, and the result is not reported in CO_2-eq, but in MJ/kg or millipoints. They range from simple tables on information cards for materials and manufacturing processes, CAD program add-ons and business systems to complex software that is oriented towards environmental experts and based on detailed data ranges.

⚠ Not every LCA tool is practical for use in different situations. Therefore, it is advisable to try the cards, spreadsheets or software tools and decide which of them are feasible.

⚠ Most LCA tools do not contain integrated information on the social impact of the chosen processes and their components. Detailed research on the potential social risks of materials and processing methods is therefore inevitable.

Deviation from the values

It will happen that, in calculations based on CO_2 equivalents, different values for the same material are found. First, the data from various databases can differ, since they operate using different indicators. Some values are already cumulative: a factor representing the processing is proportionally included in value for the material. This can vary greatly depending on where the processing takes place, as the CO_2-eq for electricity production varies greatly; for example, in Asia, it is about twice as high as the average electricity mix of the EU member states. Deviations of 30 to 50 percent can occur; therefore, missing values can also be estimated. This also applies to cost schedules. Document your assumptions; in order to make the assessment understandable, be aware of these when comparing other PCFs or LCAs. The methods offer a possibility for orientation and informed designing in a sustainable world.

⚠ LCA tools do not question the meaning of a product, nor do they give alternatives. Anyone who makes their decisions solely based on them, runs the risk of carrying out a mere eco-design, and only designing greener products, but making no relevant contribution to the sustainable development of the planet.

A detailed LCA and CO_2 footprint enable a reasoned decision for or against a proposed strategy to be made. If we compare the result with the world models of computation, we can therefore say whether the strategy is sustainable or not. It is helpful to review existing policies to see whether it is worthwhile to continue in the same direction in the future. Automakers, for example, provide information about the CO_2 footprint of their vehicles in the so-called environmental ratings. A small car with fuel-saving technology produces over its whole life cycle 25 tons of CO_2-eq over a total range of 150,000 km. If we assume that the car is driven 15,000 km a year for ten years, it therefore emits 2.5 tons of CO_2-eq per year.

From the global computation models, we know that a sustainable lifestyle should only emit one ton of CO_2-eq per year. The same type of car, available as an electric vehicle running on green energy, produces 7 tons of CO_2-eq during its life cycle, or 0.7 tons CO_2-eq per year. Even in this optimized case, an environmentally compatible way of life would leave only 0.3 tons CO_2-eq per year for the entire remaining life of its user. Such environmental ratings must therefore be considered unsustainable, even if we would like to believe the supposed accolades.

⚠ Although manufacturers provide LCAs, sustainability is not correctly interpreted politically or by the market! The science of environmental assessment must shed its white coat and make its results clearly understandable by laymen, consumers and designers alike.

We still lack an independent organization that manages, compiles and publishes data on the environmental and social impacts of materials and processes! Nevertheless, the argument of being ignorant about these effects is not valid today. Increasingly, companies use environmental management systems. These are an integral part of the business management systems that are already in use for the environmental certification of enterprises. Whoever wants to have a say in the future must be aware of the contexts.

5

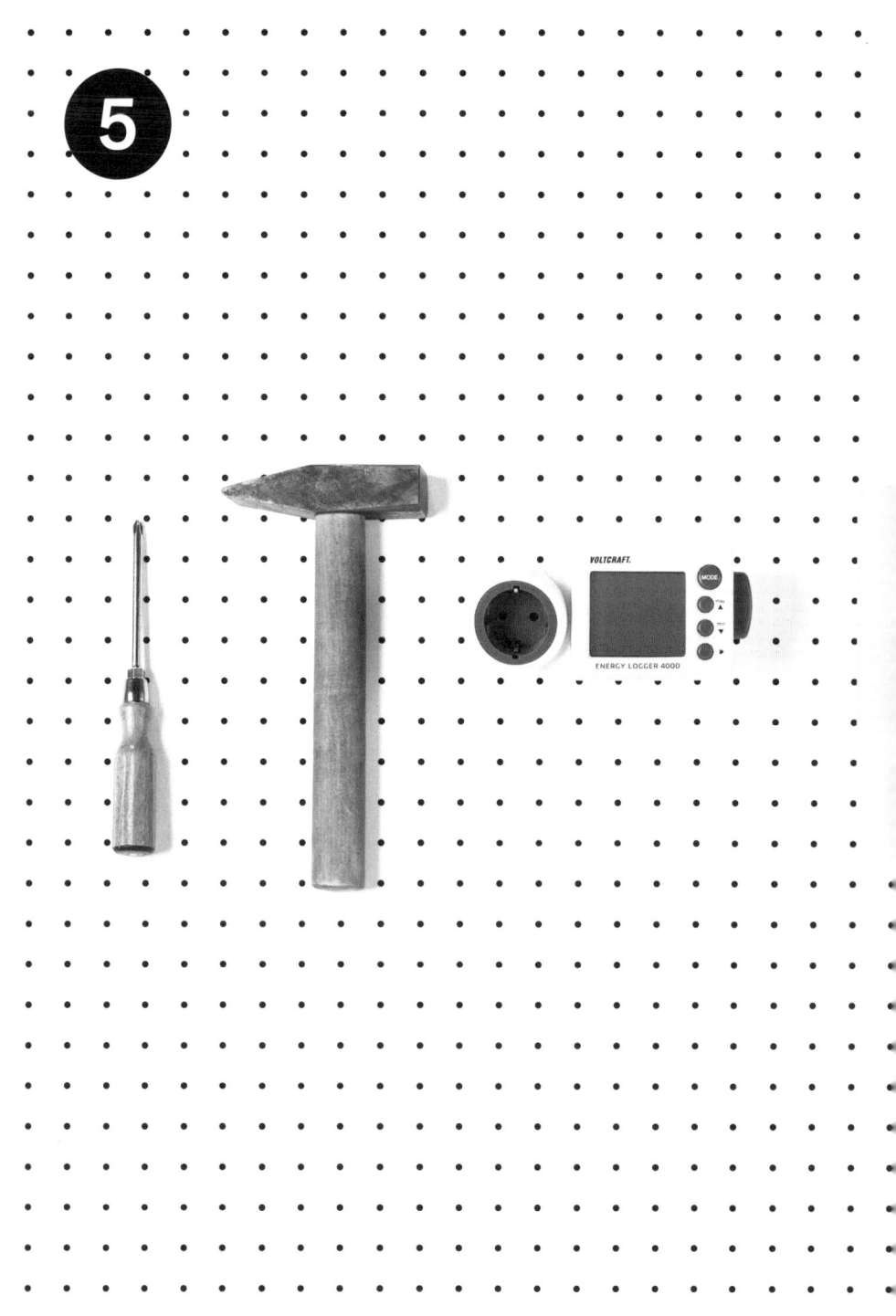

exacta

Tools for the Design Revolution   65

⑤ Universal Tools

Everything you need to make well-informed design, production or consumption decisions quickly and easily can be found in the universal tool box

Hammer

The hammer is a symbol of the working class. It is suitable to be held in the air symbolically, or – in our case – to bang items that you cannot disassemble with other tools into parts for analysis. When we need it, something has probably gone wrong in design or construction, or the manufacturers want to try to prevent the disassembly of an object.

Screwdriver

The screwdriver is the nicer way to disassemble things. But you can also use it in combination with the hammer for targeted, brutal tactics in order to separate otherwise non-detachable joints once and for all. Good design brings screws back!

Kitchen scale

It is advisable to use as precise a scale as possible, otherwise the results of the calculations could be very inaccurate. A postal scale or a dietary scale is very good for smaller items. But there is nothing wrong with an accurate mechanical scale. In any case, you should be able to see one to two gram increments clearly; otherwise it is impossible to evaluate small amounts of material.

Ammeter

There are now for sale at hardware stores very simple and cheap electricity meters. It is only important that they are suitable for 220/110 volts AC and can monitor the energy consumed in kWh (kilowatt hours). Local utilities sometimes provide such ammeters for free allowing you to measure the consumption of electricity – and as we have seen, power consumption is often the greatest environmental impact of electrical devices.

Unfortunately, however, you cannot measure whether the electricity is generated from renewable resources.

Paper and pencil

The design revolution needs tools that are available everywhere. A computer is not absolutely necessary when you have a sheet of paper and writing tools.

Pocket calculator

Actually, we only need the basic arithmetic operations: add and subtract, multiply and divide. There can be quite a few decimal places, and for these cases, a simple calculator is handy, but not essential. We find arithmetic important because it is the only possible way to come to objective conclusions. This also makes it possible to identify the environmental impacts in a life cycle where improvements would have a significant influence on the overall result.

⚠ A gut feeling is often deceptive in the evaluation of environmentally relevant factors. The parameters that we consider to be important influencing factors emotionally are not always significant.

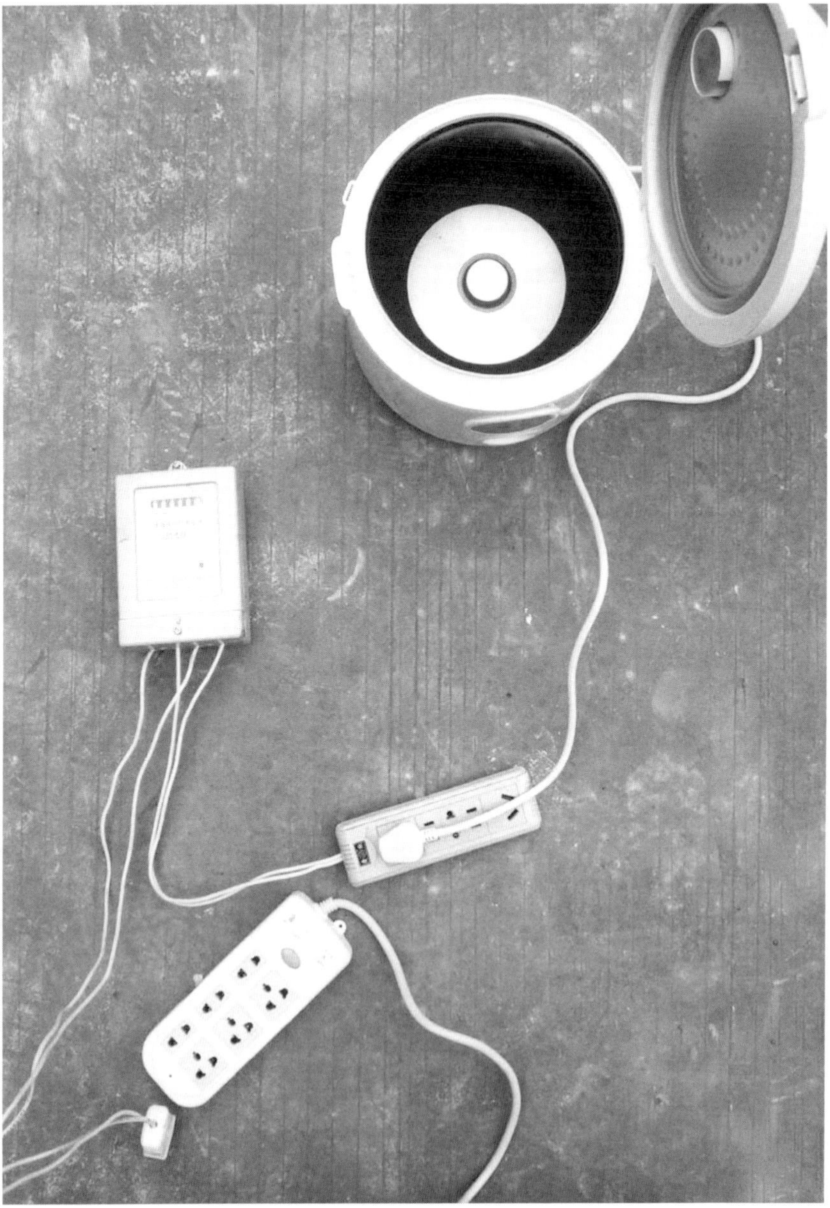

We probably have all of these tools at home or in the office already. We certainly have a current meter – but that is usually sealed and should remain where it is. Once at a workshop of the IDRV at the Southwest Jiatong University in Chengdu – probably due to a translation error – the students removed a sealed meter in order to equip the revolution box. The scale was a Chinese apothecary scale – a simple beam balance, but one that can also measure very small weights.

Since it is so easy to get the necessary tools, there is no excuse not to have an idea about the impact of a product or a service over its entire life cycle. Even if it seems almost too easy, these tools are in fact sufficient for the analysis. They are equally suitable to be used in large or small companies as well as in training contexts such as schools or universities.

(+) An always-ready box of tools reminds us of their use! This is the first-aid kit for the design of the future.

5.1 A Recipe for an LCA

A quick design life cycle analysis of light bulbs

1 incandescent light bulb, 60 watts (1,000 hour lifespan) with packaging (E27, energy rating E)

1 LED light bulb, 10 watts (15,000 hour lifespan) with packaging (E27, energy rating A+)

1 kitchen scale

1 screwdriver

1 ammeter

1 calculator

1 pencil

paper for writing

characteristic values for environmental impacts (e.g. CO_2 footprint)

This recipe is easy to make at home. The consideration of environmental impacts in terms of greenhouse gas emissions can therefore be integrated in a simplified manner into the design and conception process. Lots of everyday items (still) lack a life cycle analysis. Using basic tools, it is nevertheless possible to define their environmental impacts and to plan and test significant environmental improvements.

1. After selecting a light source (e.g. a desk lamp) the incandescent bulb is screwed in. The ammeter is plugged in between the lamp's plug and the power socket, according to its instructions, then turned on to read power use (in watts) and record it.

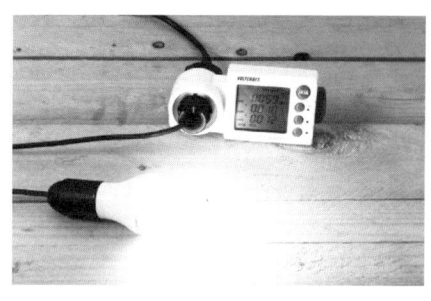

2. Repeat the same process with the LED light bulb. Check that the readings match the information on the package. For devices with a standby function, you must record the power consumption in this mode as well.

Measure electrical energy (1.–2.)

3. Carefully disassemble the glass bulb with a screwdriver. Attention! Wear protective goggles and gloves. The glass should be roughly separated from the metal. Make three piles: packaging cardboard, metal, glass.

4. Break down the LED light with the screwdriver as well. Separate the plastic, electronic converter, LED board, metal parts, insulation compound, aluminum heat sink and packaging cardboard.

5. Now weigh the individual materials with the kitchen scale and record them, preferably in kilograms (kg) on the analysis table.

Weigh and calculate footprint (5.)

Dismantle (3.)

Sort materials (4.)

6. Next to the amounts, write the factors for the different materials (see table). These are multiplied by the given amounts to get the CO₂ footprint for each respective material. The multipliers include the extraction and processing of the material. The sum of all of these items yields the footprint for the bulbs' production in the factory.

7. To calculate the footprint for the distribution, a route must be determined (based on the following assumptions): The incandescent bulb (made in Italy) is transported perhaps 1,000 kilometers by truck. The LED (made in China) is transported 15,000 km by ship and 1,000 km by truck. The distances are multiplied by the factor for transport (see table).

Environmental impact of materials

Material (1 kg)	CO₂ footprint (kg CO₂-eq)
glass	1.1
aluminum	3.7
plastic (i.e. polycarbonate)	8.0
electronics	11.5
metal (brass)	6.4
silicon	9.7
LED board	18.2
cardboard	1.0

Environmental impact of transport

Transport (1 kg material/1,000 km)	CO₂ footprint (kg CO₂-eq)
truck	0.18
ship	0.01

Data based on: PE International, GaBi – LCA software

74 Tools for the Design Revolution

8. To calculate the use phase: The lifetime (in hours) is multiplied by the amount of energy (in kilowatts: 1 watt = 0.001 kW); this gives the consumed electrical energy (kWh).

9. The electrical energy is then multiplied by the regional factor for electricity to yield the footprint for the use phase.

10. The sum of the production, distribution and use phases gives the total footprint. In a detailed life cycle analysis, recovery must also be considered. This impact is not a very high percentage, however, and will not be considered here. In order to compare the two light bulbs, the footprint must be based on, for example, 1,000 hours of use.

Environmental impact of electricity (mix by region)

Electrical energy (1 kWh)	CO_2 footprint (kg CO_2-eq)
Europe	0.36
Asia	0.77
Africa	0.70
North America	0.57
Latin America	0.19

Source: IPCC, Carbon Dioxide Intensity of Electricity

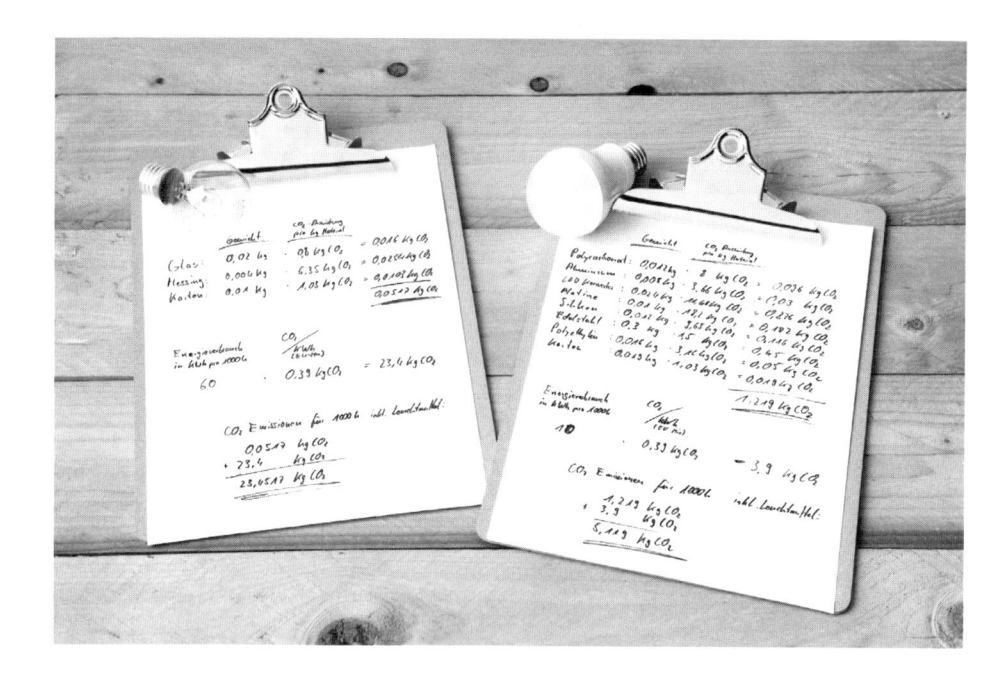

The light bulbs in comparison

	Incandescent (1,000 h)	LED (1,000 h)
manufacturing	0.05 kg CO₂-eq	1.22 kg CO₂-eq
distribution	0.01 kg CO₂-eq	0.04 kg CO₂-eq
use 1,000 h*	23.4 kg CO₂-eq	3.9 kg CO₂-eq
footprint for 1,000 h	23.46 kg CO₂-eq	5.16 kg CO₂-eq

*(EU energy mix)

At first, everything seems clear: Despite the higher CO_2 footprint in manufacturing, the LED light produces about 80 percent less CO_2 after 1,000 hours of use. Transport by ship from China hardly affects the overall balance. This solution seems sustainable, because through a change in technology, the demands for energy reduction (2,000-watt society) and a radical reduction in greenhouse gas emissions (low carbon society, 1 ton of CO_2) are already being met. The additional cost for the production of LED lights can be justified by the overall savings, as well as by its 15-fold lifespan.

Usage scenarios
The calculation does not appear so clear when green energy is used. After the footprint of the necessary infrastructure is included in the "gray" footprint, green energy without greenhouse gas emissions can be calculated. Suddenly the incandescent bulb and the LED are very similar in their CO_2 footprints. The higher power consumption of the incandescent carries no energy savings, of course, but a significant reduction in greenhouse gas emissions could still be realized here with the old technology!

⚠ The effect of usage scenarios in the energy consumption of objects is not considered and communicated enough. In this example, the switch to energy from renewable sources brings a greater savings in CO_2-eq than a technology revolution in a light source that is still powered by electricity from non-renewable sources.

⚠ Inefficient solutions are increasingly being regulated by law, or at least identified. An incandescent bulb with an efficiency of Class D is now banned in the European Union. A car with an efficiency of Class D is still free to harm the environment, however. In both cases, the industry uses its political influence to continue to make a profit at the expense of the environment.

⚠ The rebound effect: Efficient solutions often result in thoughtless use. A new LED light might never be turned off after use because it is so environmentally friendly. Thus, under certain circumstances, the savings could be cancelled out due to increased use.

⚠ A simple life cycle analysis shows that the greatest environmental impact in terms of greenhouse gases arises during the use phase. Therefore, potential savings are offered not only by a more efficient light source, but also by measures that ensure maximum efficiency for the user. With an intelligent light control, output can be dimmed or even shut down depending on the amount of daylight.

⚠ Informed design also means taking into account the fact that the light intensity decreases exponentially with the distance from the light source. It follows that, for example, desk lamps, which can be adapted to the work situation, can be more efficient than floor lamps, which illuminate the entire workspace.

5.2 A Bold Life Cycle Analysis

Recipe for the analysis of complex products

CO₂ footprint per product unit

Product (1 kg)	CO₂-footprint (kg CO₂-eq)
mobile telephone	509
laptop computer	242
automobile	5

Data based on the EPDs of the respective products.

Footprint of cars in t CO_2-eq

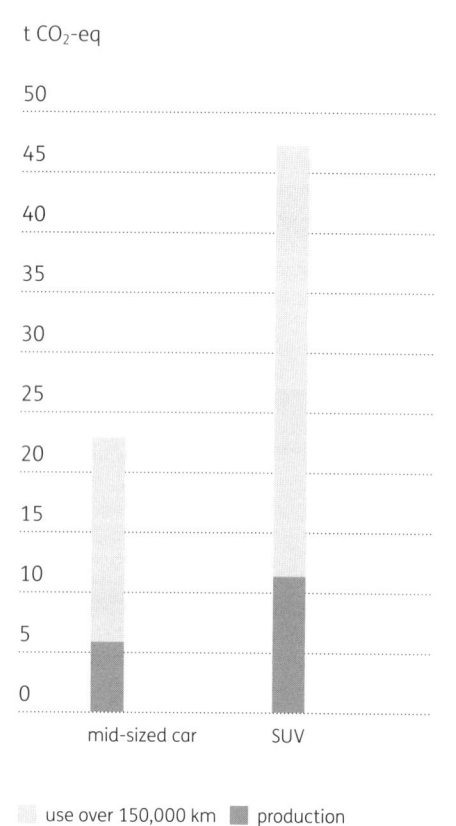

t CO_2-eq

- mid-sized car: ~20 (use over 150,000 km) + ~5 (production)
- SUV: ~45 (use over 150,000 km) + ~10 (production)

☐ use over 150,000 km   ■ production

78   Tools for the Design Revolution

Mobile phones, cars and laptops can theoretically be analyzed with the tool described above. The results may differ greatly from professionally produced LCAs, however. That is why we have developed a simple method for such cases: We do not calculate each individual material, but rather the total footprint of a category of objects. From a known life cycle assessment – for example, for a mobile phone – the CO_2 footprint for production is taken and divided by the product weight. Thus one easily gets the CO_2 footprint of a 1-kilogram mobile phone. The same method can be applied to a car, for example.

Example: Footprint of a large SUV
LCAs are not mandatory, so why should vehicle manufacturers create them for cars that do not have a good reputation in terms of their environmental impact anyway? Although there is little reason for driving SUVs in the city, this vehicle category enjoys a high popularity there nonetheless. But are these vehicles really that bad? Here, our simple method provides some clarity. According to a published LCA, a 1,200-kg midsize car emits 6 tons of CO_2-eq in production. In the glossy brochure for the SUV, a total weight of 2,297 kg is given. Multiplied by our factor of 5 yields 11.5 tons of CO_2-eq in production. The SUV emits 0.239 kg of CO_2 per kilometer. Calculated on a total range of 150,000 km yields an additional 35.8 tons of CO_2. The mid-sized car, however, has an output of 0.113 kilograms of CO_2 per kilometer, which, when projected to the same range, produces 17 tons. When it comes to transporting four people from point A to point B, the SUV emitted one hundred percent more greenhouse gases than the midsize car for the same distance.

⚠ When calculated over ten years, the production of the SUV alone caused more than 1 ton of CO_2 per year! That would already exceed a person's fair share of world pollution allowance before even one kilometer is driven. Driving 15,000 kilometers, its footprint would be 4.7 tons per year.

⚠ The SUV's greenhouse gas emissions of 0.239 kg of CO_2 per kilometer correspond to the per-kilometer emissions of a passenger on an airplane!

⊕ Alternative concepts can also be calculated and verified using this simple method. If ten people were to use one vehicle (car sharing), the production footprint (for a midsize car) per person per year would be no more than 60 kilograms. So each person saves more than half a ton of greenhouse gas per year compared to an individual user.

⚠ Fossil fuels are not suitable for powering automobiles. Even small cars that use them produce more than one ton of greenhouse gas per year (0.08 kg CO_2 per kilometer at 15,000 kilometers per year). For the whole world, this simply does not compute.

6

80 Tools for the Design Revolution

⑥ Coffee Box

"It is extremely likely that human influence has been the dominant cause of the observed warming since the mid 20th century."

IPCC, 2013:7

Club culture: of open and closed systems
Coffee has entered the world of the consumer fetish; these days, we can buy it in exclusive boutiques. Thanks to extremely large advertising expenses, every child today knows that an espresso needs a "crema". In slow motion, the last drop of coffee falls into the cup and springs back. The guarantor of this exclusive coffee experience is a proprietary capsule system. Modern man has now turned the preparation of an espresso into an alienated experience as well, in which not even a button has to be pressed! We can neither see, touch nor smell the essential good that allows us this enjoyment. Espresso as a cultural good has been transcended by the ingenuity of industry into an experience. Gone is the screwing, unscrewing, fumbling, spilling and especially the waiting. Now everybody can make a perfect espresso. A perfect espresso, not only in Italy, but all over the world: in the hospital, at the hairdresser, with Grandma and Grandpa, in the office and of course at home.

Only anti-progressive contemporaries can have reservations against this groundbreaking innovation. Is social cohesion not the agenda of the design of the future? The coffee club as a social institution of the world's salvation, ennobled by the logos of numerous NGOs. There is no doubt that everything is controlled, environmentally friendly and fair. And for the last doubters there are numbers and facts. The entire life cycle, from coffee cultivation to the recycling of the capsules, is documented in a life cycle analysis of over a hundred pages. And to break down the complex interrelationships, there is even a simple, colorful bar graph to help ease the coffee connoisseur's conscience.

"Welcome! Step into the world of …" This is the greeting from the national manager of the coffee world in a book that accompanies a revolutionary espresso machine. This world is of course marked by carefully selected knowledge about sustainability. The enemies of the exclusive coffee clubs have already expressed their objections to the elaborate packaging of pre-portioned coffee many times. But the capsule systems were of course not only optimized for perfect enjoyment, but in consideration of the ecological aspects as well. As evidence, in the manufacturer's exclusive coffee boutique, a multi-page brochure with fold-out pages is at hand. Golden shimmering capsules on a coffee-colored background tell of their immortality. Of course they are collected by the club members and brought to collection points, which is probably part of the club's code of honor. From there they go to a raw material recycler, because both the capsule and the coffee grounds are valuable raw materials. From the coffee grounds energy can be generated, and the aluminum is melted down again, naturally. This is known to be smarter and more energy efficient than producing new aluminum, as guaranteed by the joint venture of European aluminum manufacturers!

The halo of recycling formed by the two semi-circular arrows lends a sacred aura of purity to the capsule. In this world there are no environmental sins. The last page of the environmental catechism states the following: "Aluminum is simply melted down for recycling. This process is characterized by multiple advantages: very low energy consumption, no weight or quality loss and unlimited repeatability." Anyone who believes that is, at best, uninformed. A quality loss is unavoidable, since the capsules are not monomaterial, nor are they sorted before being melted down. And the coffee God errs in claiming that no weight loss would result. In industrial practice, one ton of melted aluminum scrap only yields about 850 kg of recycled aluminum. And only the capsules that end up in the collection system can be melted down. Assuming a desired collection rate of 75 percent, the recycling halo fades very quickly. Instead of eternal life, there is the quick death of the aluminum. (Resurrection ↗)

After the first use, seven out of ten capsules are recycled, but after the fifth use, that number drops to one. This is the cycle in the real world.

The flight into a different coffee world with different capsules brings no salvation. The environmental impact per every espresso drank is just as bad when it comes to the CO_2 footprint. And in a world where water is becoming increasingly scarce, an individual's water allotment is an important factor. For the 40 milliliters of espresso running into the cup, it takes almost 400 gallons of water for coffee production and aluminum capsule manufacturing! The exclusive capsule packaging weighs in at about 350 liters of water itself.

⚠ Contemporary design is no longer just about products, but the combination of products and service concepts. Sharing and usage instead of ownership are common keywords as part of a positive development in today's consumer behavior in the global North. Service offerings that have certain products being used communally have become more and more popular in recent years. This distributes the footprint of the production of an item among multiple users. New communities defined by communal usage arise, shaping their lifestyle in terms of a sustainable way of life.

⚠ Unfortunately, there are product-service concepts that multiply the environmental impact. The followers of these consumer communities are communalized into "clubs" and consider aluminum to be lifestyle waste. By purchasing a capsule coffee machine, for example, one becomes a member of the club.

This is a revised version of the text "Kommt's nur auf die Crema an?", in the insert *Spectrum* IX of *Die Presse*, 14 Dec 2013

Who wins?

Two coffee machines in comparison

A capsule coffee machine
The model of the capsule machine for preparing coffee is from the year 2013, and is described by the manufacturer as having the following characteristics: Motorized brewing unit with fully automatic capsule ejection, three programmable coffee amounts, automatic pre-selection of the preferred cup size, adaptable and removable water tank and cup rack, 25 second warm-up time and auto shut-off after 9 minutes; weight: 3 kg, tank capacity: 0.8 L, cord: 1 m, pressure: 19 bar and an output of 1,260 watts.
The patented system is from the 1970s, but only became successful through advertising campaigns with an American director and actor.

If an out-of-service capsule machine were properly delivered to the dump, for example, in Vienna, it would end up on the table of a dismantling and recycling center. Here only the cable, with a material value of about 75 cents at the current price of copper, would be cut off as the most valuable part, and the rest would go into the mixed scrap. The quantities of recyclable materials are so low that only mechanical shredding is worthwhile, and the machine is therefore assigned in tattered pieces into different material fractions at a high energy expenditure. Another scenario is thermal utilization, since the plastics cannot be recycled in any meaningful way so far.

⚠ We have found things at the junkyard surprisingly often that apparently do not have a long life, such as electric capsule coffee machines.

In preparing a cup of coffee, about 0.0023 kWh of electricity, 5 g of coffee and 40 mL of water are consumed. It takes two minutes for the coffee to get to the cup. There is also the packaging: 1 aluminum capsule.

Bialetti Moka Express
The Bialetti Moka Express, designed by Alfonso Bialetti, has been produced almost unchanged since 1933. With the Moka Express, a coffeemaker was invented that enables a cup of coffee just like in a café to be prepared at home without any technical skills. At that time in Italy it was a social innovation and a symbol of the dawn of the modern age; before then, coffee was usually drunk only in public. The Moka Express can be operated with any heat source, whether it is gas or electric, and can be filled with a variety of ground coffees according to taste. We can only estimate the lifespan of a Moka Express, but since it is very robust and the parts that are subject to wear and tear, such as a rubber gasket or a valve, are available as replacement parts in any well-stocked household goods store, some machines probably outlast their original owners.

They are popular treasures at flea markets. Because the Moka Express is made of 98% aluminum, it could even be recycled as aluminum scrap.

To prepare a cup of coffee using an electric hot plate, 0.0030 kWh of electricity, 5 g of coffee and 40 mL of water are consumed. It takes eight minutes for the coffee to reach the cup.

88 Tools for the Design Revolution

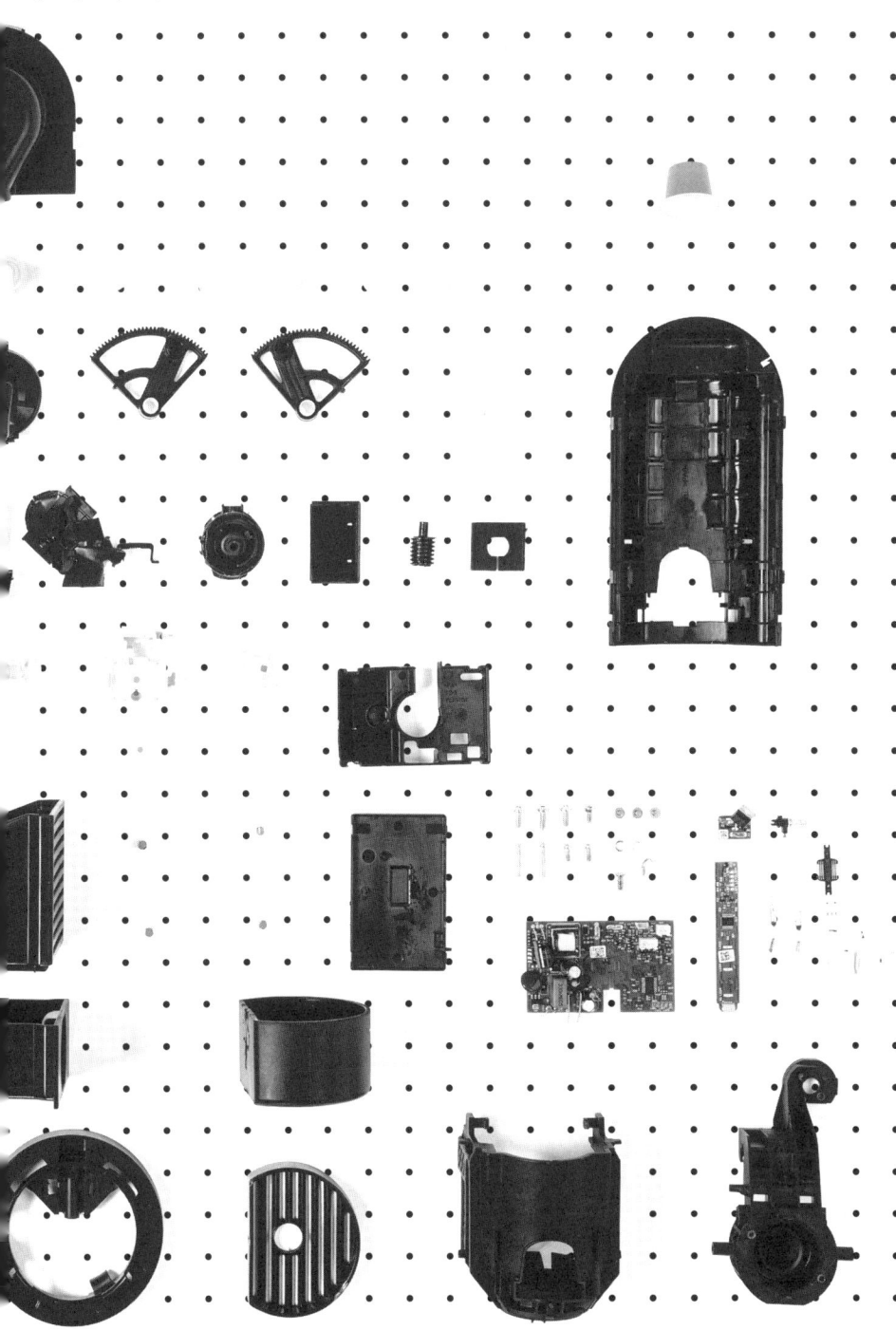

Tools for the Design Revolution   89

90   Tools for the Design Revolution

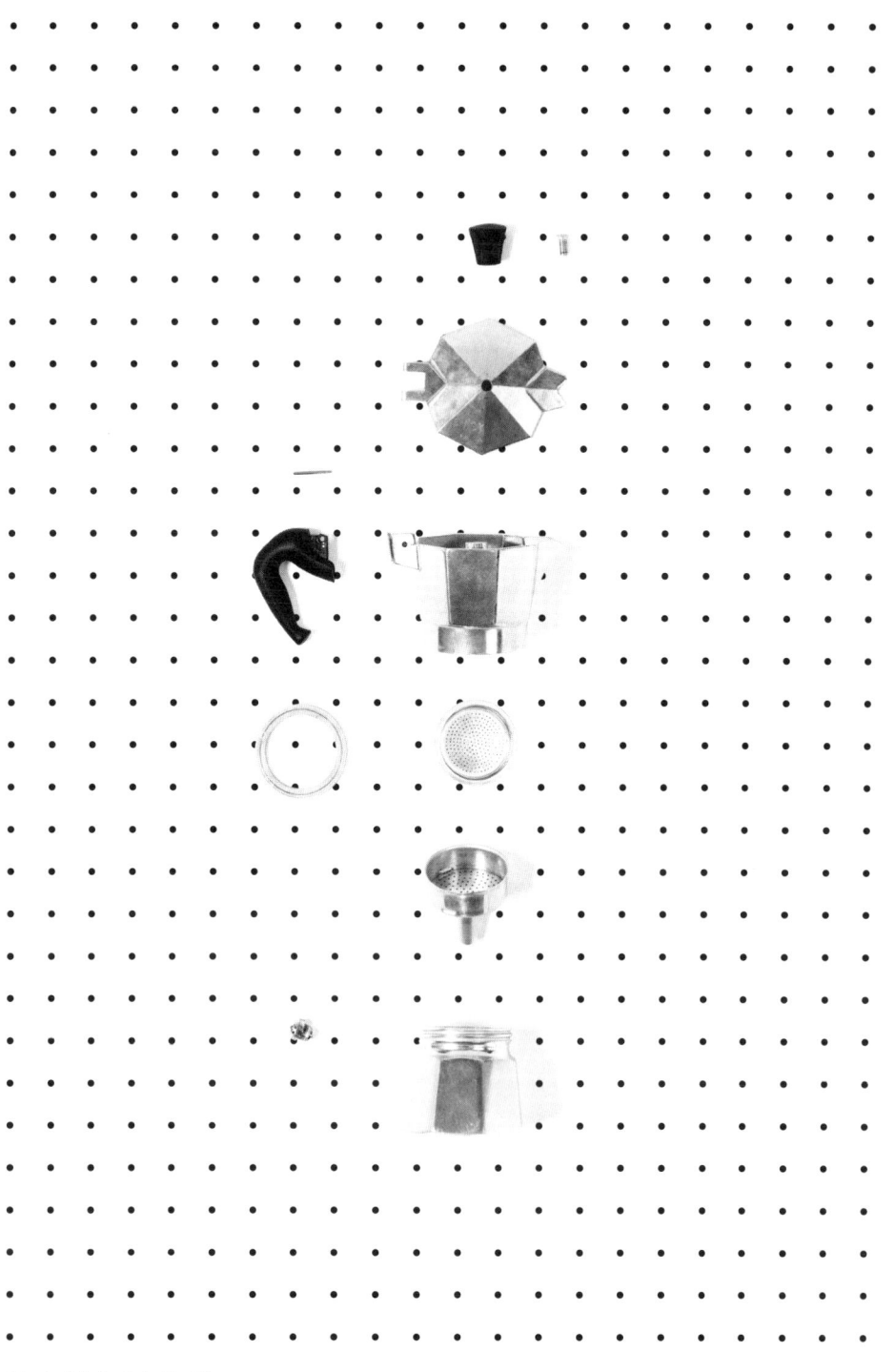

The machines in detail

Using the universal tools, the two different coffee preparation products are broken down and weighed.

Capsule machine

After more than two hours of work on the capsule machine, we get the following values:

ABS plastic	0.735 kg
PBT6F / other plastic	0.06 kg
PA 6	0.143 kg
PA66GF	0.22 kg
plexiglas / acrylic	0.18 kg
rubber / silicon	0.017 kg
copper	0.015 kg
circuit board	0.05 kg
electronics	0.771 kg
aluminum capsule	0.003 kg
steel	0.11 kg
insulation	0.044 kg
magnets	0.003 kg
chrome	0.003 kg

Moka Express

Disassembling the Moka Express yields the following amounts of material:

aluminum	0.218 kg
plastic	0.018 kg
rubber	0.006 kg
stainless steel	0.009 kg
cardboard	0.07 kg

With the help of the universal tools, the two different coffee preparation products can be disassembled and weighed. For comparison, it is assumed that both machines have been in use for four years and have prepared 3,000 cups of coffee. Both products are produced in Europe and travel about 700 km by truck from the production site to the retail store in Vienna. For an electrical power mix, EU-27 is average.

⚠ The electronic components of the capsule machines likely come from a supplier, but we have no exact data on this, which is why the European production site is defined as a system boundary.

Unlike the Moka Express, the coffee capsule machine can only be opened with special tools – therefore the hammer has to be used. Some materials and electronic components are glued and cannot be put back together. The device is now useless in its original function.

Disassembling the two coffee preparation products makes the different material costs clear. Measuring the electrical current shows that the capsule machine uses less power to prepare a cup of coffee. Only the LCA provides information on which method has a better environmental balance over the entire life cycle.

The material quantities are assigned environmental impact factors using the Ecolizer 2.0, a design tool by Ovam. There are also values from the production phase that are used in this case.
After inserting the factors and calculating according to the life cycles, a bar chart can be generated in a spreadsheet program, providing information on the overall impact over the various phases of the life cycle.

Life Cycle Comparison (mPt)

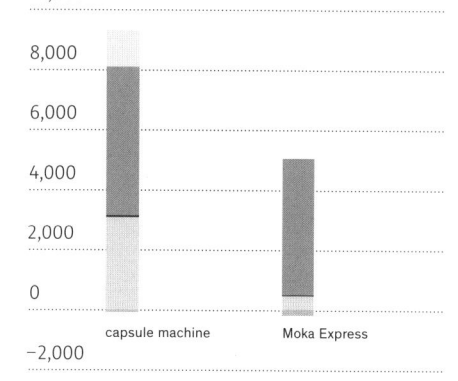

mPt after
Ecolizer 2.0

10,000
8,000
6,000
4,000
2,000
0
−2,000

capsule machine — Moka Express

- aluminum capsule
- use
- distribution
- manufacturing
- end of life

According to the guidelines of a simplified LCA, using the numbers from the universal toolbox, the results can be compared in the form of CO_2 footprints.
The insertion of the CO_2-eq factors yields the following diagram:

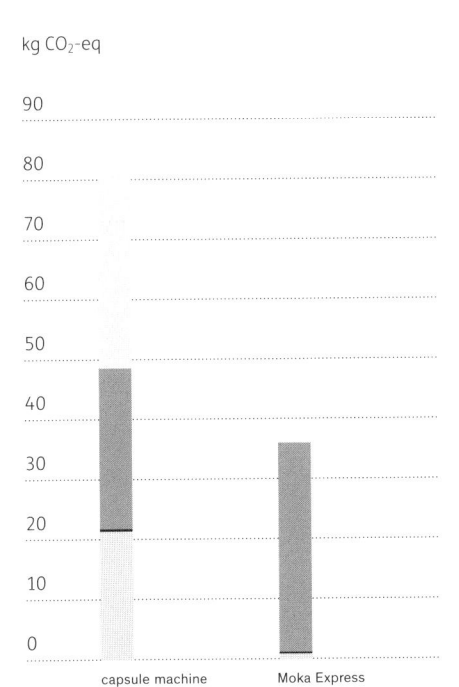

Both diagrams show a similar result. Capsule preparation has an environmental impact that is about twice as high as the more than 80-year-old method. The higher expenditure of energy in the use of the Moka Express is small in comparison with the material overhead in the production of the capsule machines. In addition, the capsule machine still suffers from the coffee portion packaging, which has one of the highest environmental impacts of all factors. The gain in comfort is paid for with a footprint that's twice as large.

Life Cycle Comparison (CO_2-eq)

kg CO_2-eq

(Bar chart showing capsule machine at ~45 and Moka Express at ~35)

- aluminum capsule
- use
- distribution
- manufacturing

It's all about the content
So far, however, we have not dealt with what is really at stake in the analysis: the coffee.

Before it reaches the consumer, ground coffee is responsible for about 30 g of CO_2-eq per cup (5g). 3,000 cups of coffee alone cause the release of 90 kg of CO_2-eq. The reasoning behind the aluminum packaging is that it best protects the coffee and ensures the highest quality. It is right in principle to protect the precious commodity of the beans from destruction or loss of quality, because coffee is the essential product. Looking at the whole value chain of a cup of coffee, the coffee bean itself has the highest proportional CO_2 footprint. The example of the coffee capsule machine is a purely technical solution, which attempts to produce quality at a high material cost. However, a conversation with a coffee expert revealed to us that the coffee in the capsules is neither particularly good nor fairly traded. And the advantage of perfect storage can also be achieved if some already known household instructions are followed.

⚠ Always store the beans dry at room temperature; do not buy packages that are too large and keep resealing them. And the best aromas result if the beans are ground immediately before brewing.

With a price per kilo of up to 70 euros, we seem to be willing to spend for coffee from the capsule machine 3 to 4 times the price of excellent and fairly produced coffee. Much of the price of coffee is caused by speculation on the stock market and goes to people who never had the raw materials in their own hands. Even with coffee designated as "fair trade," only a fraction of the price per kilo is earned by the coffee farmers. If we were to buy the coffee at this price per kilo from the farmers directly, it would provide them with a decent wage. There are already initiatives to import and roast the beans through smaller intermediaries, and to use part of the proceeds for the construction of schools so that the children have another option besides toiling on the plantations.

⚠ Technical innovations are a way to improve and maintain the apparent quality of a raw material. In the example of the capsule system, it is obvious that this means a high and wasteful use of other valuable resources. In this case, it is not sustainable. An alternative is to disseminate knowledge on the production and preparation of coffee. Whoever is informed about the production and preparation methods, and is able to decide for themselves where he gets his coffee, can deal with the resource consciously. Quality is characterized not by a high price alone. It results from the valuation and honest dealing between the producers and the consumers.

⚠ Using existing infrastructure: The Moka Express uses the existing kitchen infrastructure, reducing the resource consumption per product. Some coffee drinkers are committed to the French press or filter cup preparation methods, which work even more resource-efficiently with water heated in a kettle.

⚠ Time factor: The coffee capsule machine is six minutes faster in preparation than the Moka Express. However, coffee drinking used to be seen in all cultures as a social ceremony which no one measures with a stopwatch. In addition, coffee has traditionally not been drunk alone. Methods that allowed the enjoyment of coffee at home were a great innovation. But where does this development lead today? Innovation is too often understood today as something that promotes efficiency, allowing people to do anything anywhere at any time. Thus we are able to conduct even more business and consume even more – creating a hamster wheel.

⚠ Design as a cultural discipline must be aware of the traditional rites that have evolved over many centuries.

7

makezine.com

THE MAKER'S BILL OF RIGHTS

- Meaningful and specific parts lists shall be included.
- Cases shall be easy to open. ■ Batteries shall be replaceable. ■ Special tools are allowed only for darn good reasons. ■ Profiting by selling expensive special tools is wrong, and not making special tools available is even worse. ■ Torx is OK; tamperproof is rarely OK.
- Components, not entire subassemblies, shall be replaceable. ■ Consumables, like fuses and filters, shall be easy to access. ■ Circuit boards shall be commented.
- Power from USB is good; power from proprietary power adapters is bad. ■ Standard connectors shall have pinouts defined. ■ If it snaps shut, it shall snap open. ■ Screws better than glues. ■ Docs and drivers shall have permalinks and shall reside for all perpetuity at archive.org. ■ Ease of repair shall be a design ideal, not an afterthought. ■ Metric or standard, not both.
- Schematics shall be included.

Make: technology on your time

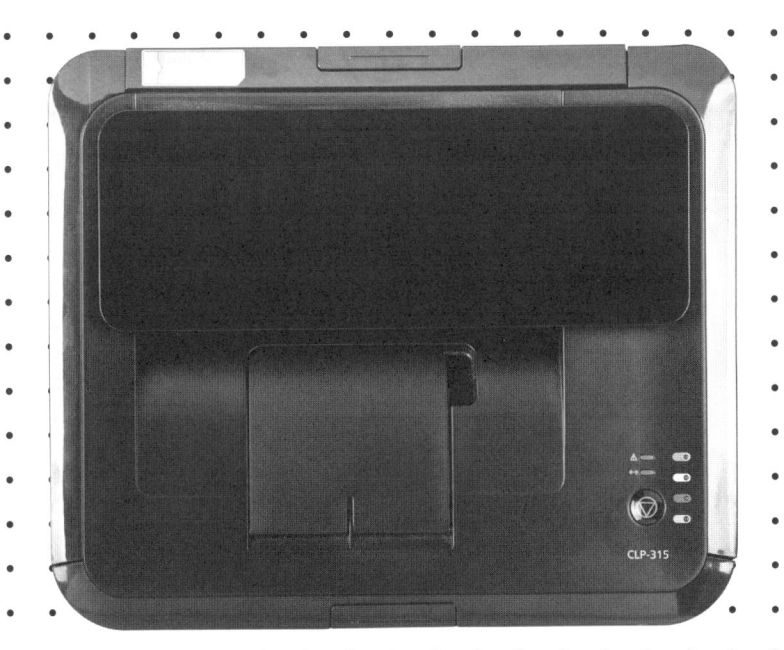

Tools for the Design Revolution

⑦ Quick Death

On cartridge containers, the repair revolution and images of resistance

In an abstract way, a gun and a printer can both be a "container" for cartridges. In both cases, this container is designed in such a way that it includes the triggering mechanism for activating the cartridges. For laser and inkjet printers, counters are installed in these containers, which, for example, report that the cartridge is spent after the 15,000th printed page.

⚠ A warning light on the printer flashes: TONER LOW. But I just changed the cartridge … Does this sound familiar?

This measure is known as "planned wearout" or "planned obsolescence" and it means that the lifespan of a product is intentionally shortened by the manufacturer – by manipulating counters, building in vulnerabilities, using inferior quality materials, or also by shortening fashion cycles – which should stimulate a new purchase. So half-full cartridges are thrown away; washing machines that function in principle are disposed of because repairs are more expensive than a new device; a new phone is bought every other year with the promise of additional features; old refrigerators are replaced with energy-efficient ones, and so on. This economic incentive structure was developed in the 1920s at General Motors, which introduced automobiles to the market in new configurations every year. Thus, customers should be made to buy new cars after three years. Today, planned obsolescence is practiced in various forms and in almost all industries.

⚠ Placing the AK-47 and the printer side by side raises the question: Is it conceivable that the arms industry would give their products counters that indicate a weapon is useless after 15,000 shots? Probably not. This product would most likely not be purchased by belligerent powers. So why in our peaceful life do we constantly buy "for the dump"? (Dannoritzer, Reuß: References ↗)

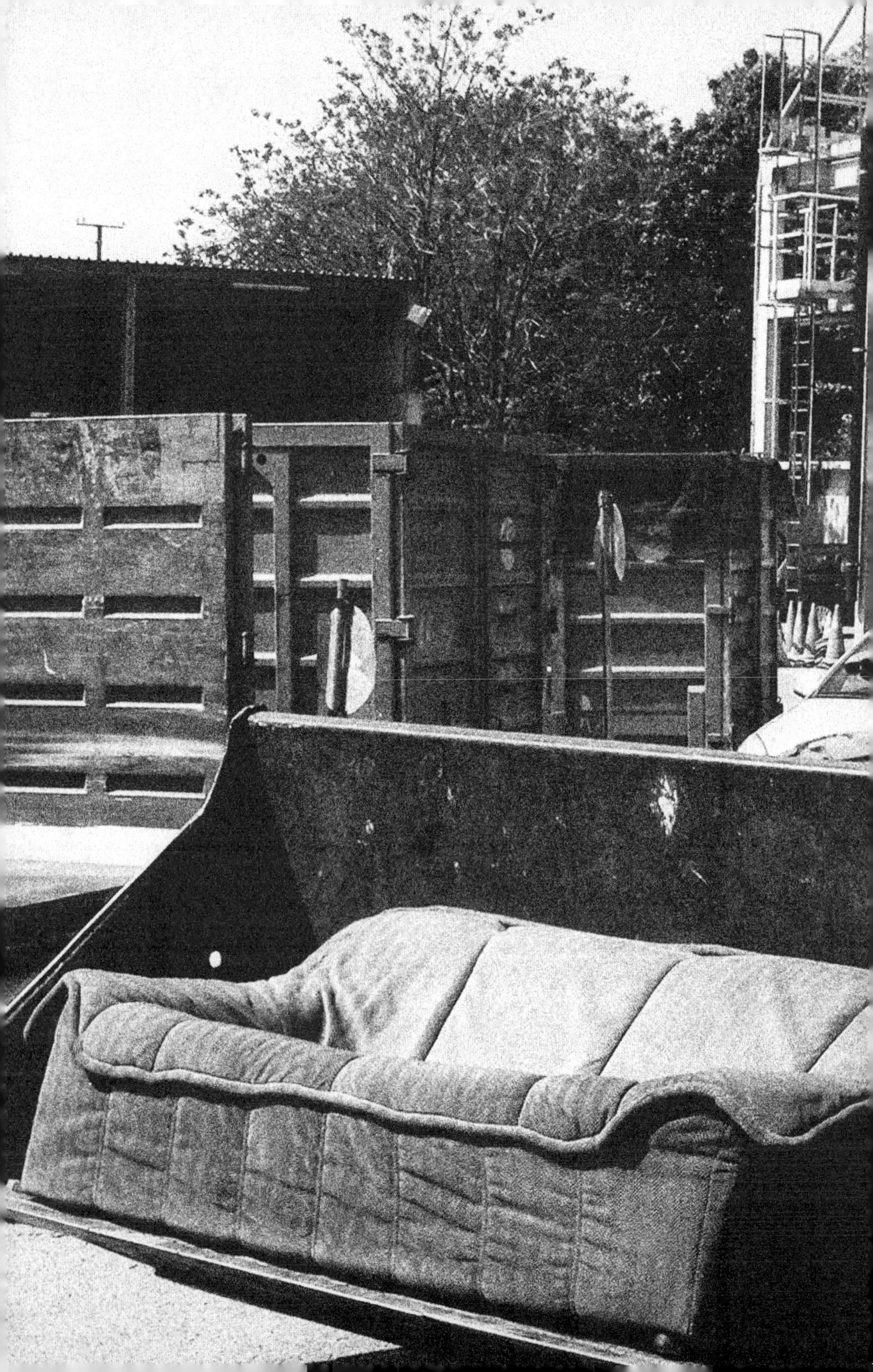

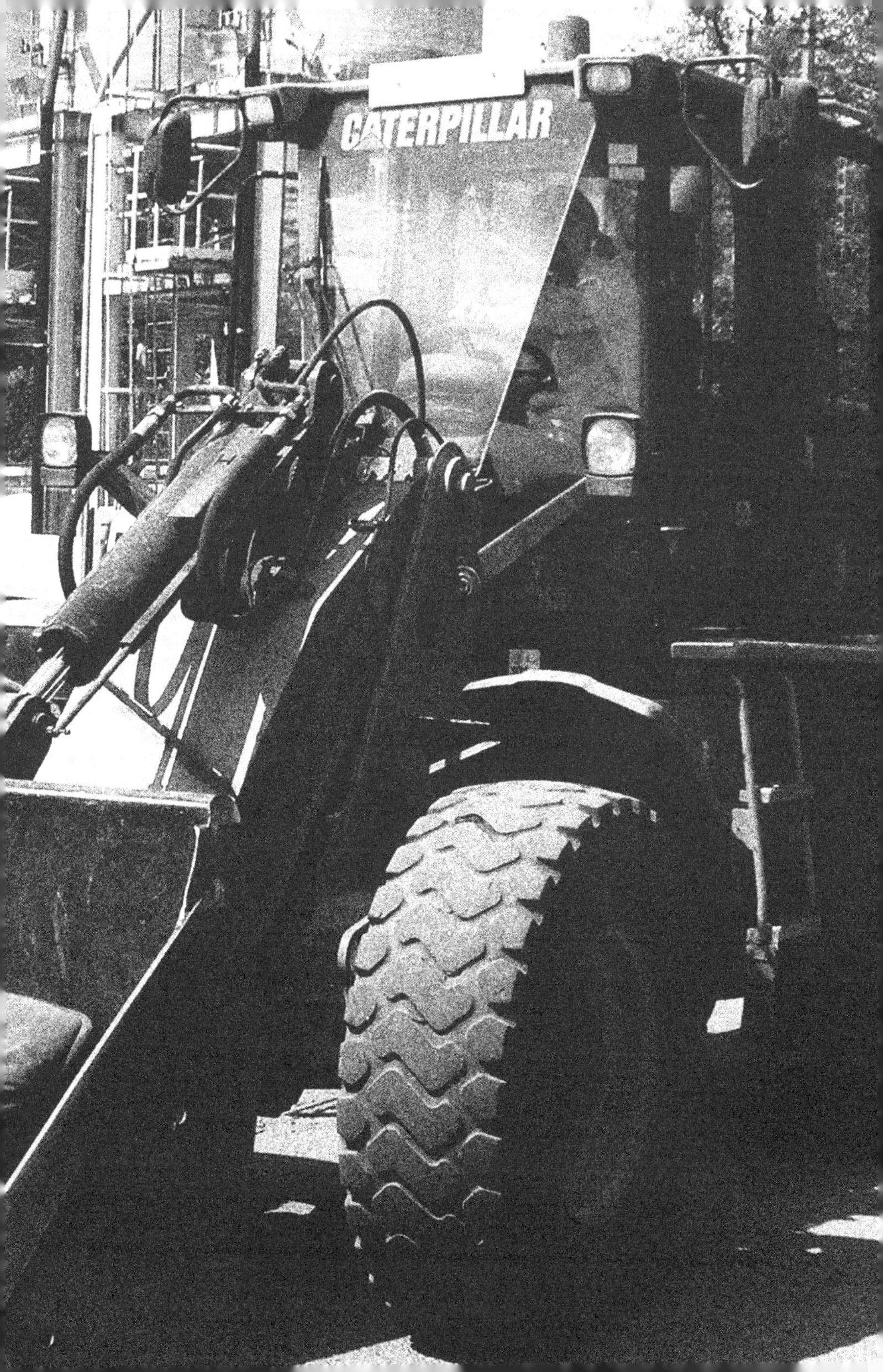
CATERPILLAR

"It is considered good manufacturing practice, and not bad ethics, occasionally to change designs so that old models will become obsolete and new ones will have the chance to be bought. […] We have been told […] that this is clever business, that the object of business ought to be to get people to buy frequently and that it is bad business to try to make anything that will last forever, because when once a man is sold a car he will not buy again. Our principle of business is precisely the opposite.

We cannot conceive how to serve the consumer unless we make for him something that, so far as we can provide, will last forever. […] It does not please us to have a buyer's

car wear out or become obsolete.
We want the man who buys
one of our cars never to have to buy
another. We never make an
improvement that renders any
previous model obsolete."

Henry Ford, 1922 (Slade, 2007:32f.)

Henry Ford's quote from the 1920s shows hints of what is still the fundamental conflict of the prevailing economic system: the primacy of the company (business) over ethics (morality), and the primacy of economic growth over all other areas of the life and the environment. Moreover, Ford's quality and durability principles would not prove to be economical. But they are more relevant now than ever, and at the same time, they imply the call for a post-growth economy.

Cartridge containers: the printer

A laser printer is an example of how a product's premature end of life is planned during manufacturing. It contains some components that can be manipulated and used by manufacturers to ensure the need for new printers, thus ensuring that their sales remain constant or increase. A gear-driven counter mechanism ascertains how many pages have been printed. This information – stored on inconspicuous chips – is used to determine the status of the cartridge. From the outside, the level is not visible, and when the printer says the cartridge is empty, we switch it out – even though we can still print several pages with it. After a few cartridges have been replaced, there are further reports of a contaminated or defective print head. The device's predetermined time of death has been reached. According to the service information, it is not worth repairing, because a new device is already available for a few euros more.

In this way, technically faultless equipment ends up in the garbage every day. On the devices, glaring signs warn against opening the product. The warranty is voided as soon as the first screw is loosened – provided that the appropriate special screwdriver could ever be found. Manufacturers have managed to instill in us the feeling that we would be committing a crime if, against all advice and recommendations, we attempted to take life-prolonging measures on our printers. But who is to say how we should behave? And is it wrong to undermine the dictates of industry?

The cartridge

We can easily refuel a car again when the tank is empty – it's a matter of course. This could also be a matter of course for printer cartridges – whether toner or ink cartridges – in the form of a trade-in service or independently at home. It would only require one of the many how-to videos circulating on the Internet, a pad to protect the surrounding area from ink stains and some technical skills. In addition to positive effects for the environment, we could save on the relatively expensive ink, which the printer manufacturers use to recover the costs of the cheap devices.

Tools for the Design Revolution 105

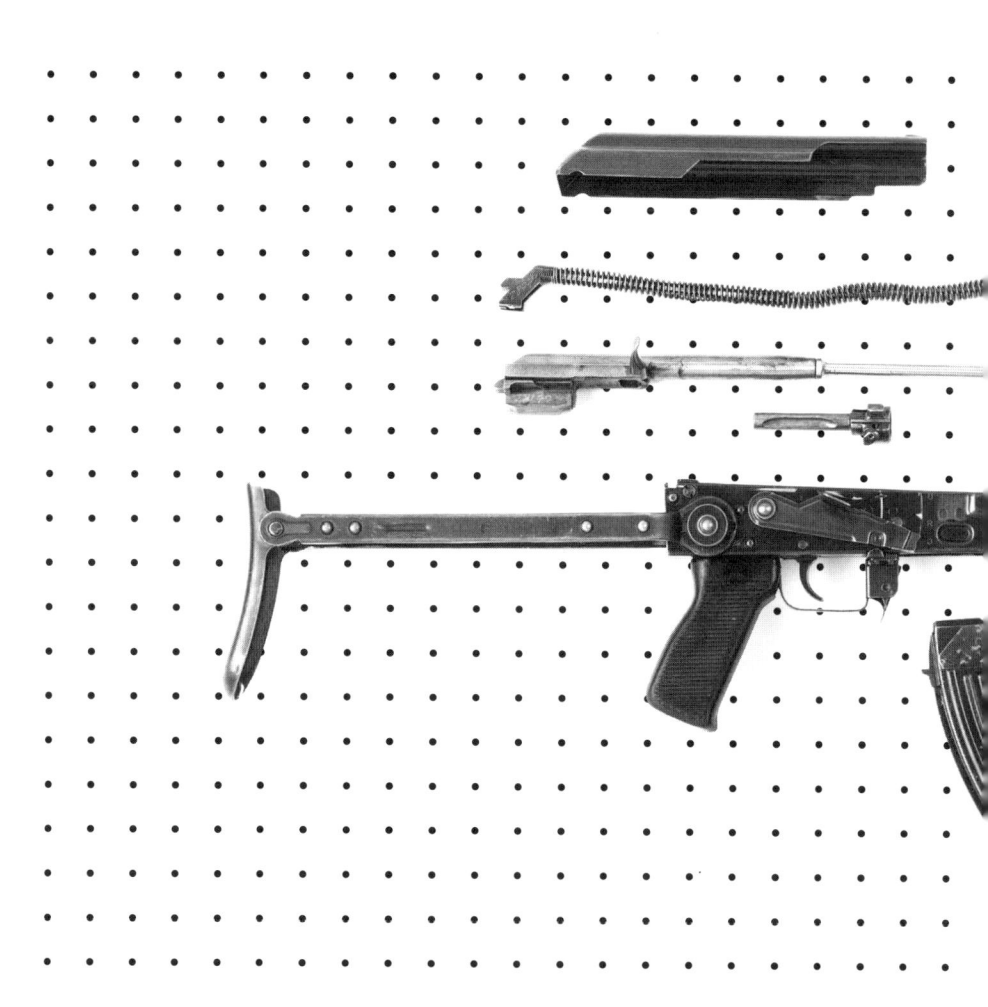

The Kalashnikov AK-47
fulfills some of the basic principles for sustainable design: it consists of few materials, it is easy to use, is easy to disassemble into parts, it is not glued together and it uses standardized parts. The spare parts are readily available, it is easy to repair, it is robust and very durable and it is made of easily recyclable material. These criteria suggest that no planned wearout is scheduled.

Its robustness and simple user experience have made the rapid-fire rifle, which was originally developed for the Soviet armed forces after the Second World War, and its replicas the standard weapon for many official armed forces as well as various unofficial fighters. Today it is the most widely used rifle in the world, making the procurement of spare parts and ammunition extremely simple.

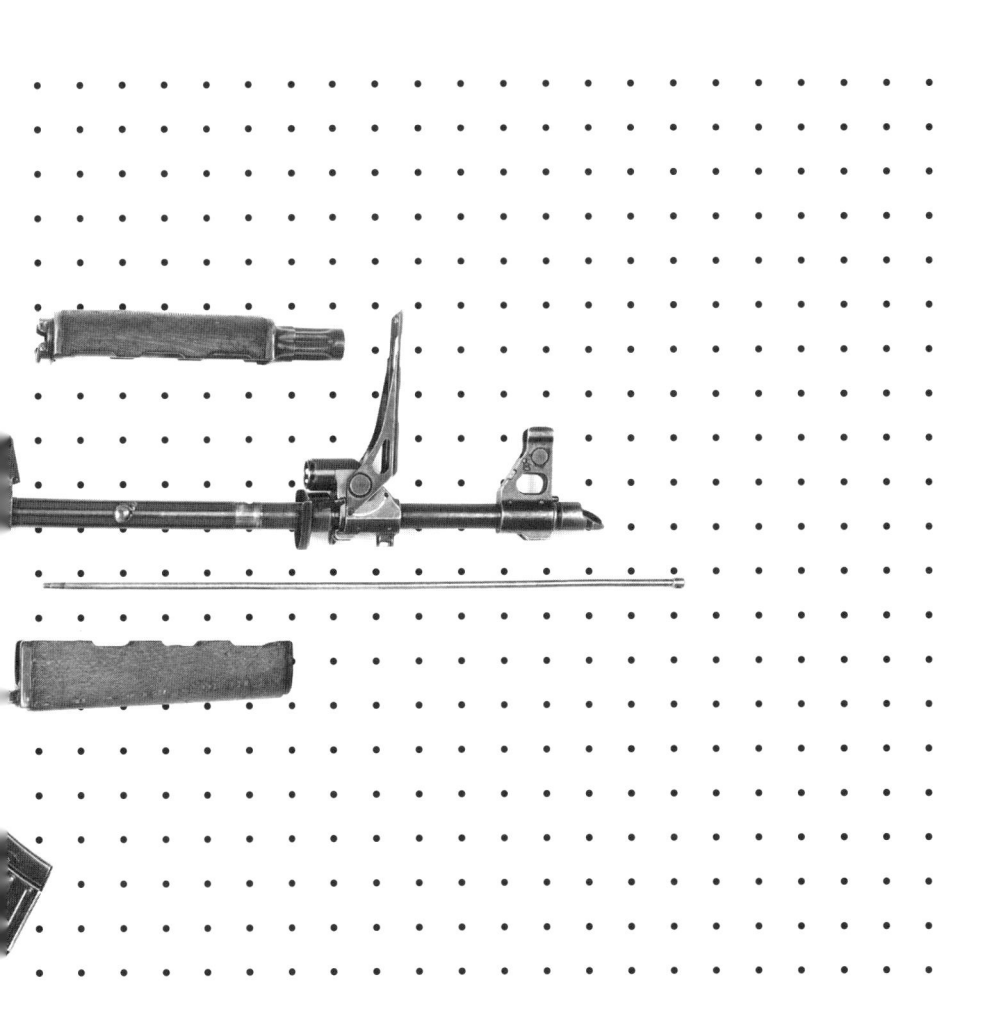

Its unregulated proliferation has caused the deaths of thousands of people every year – most of them civilians, including many children.

The Kalashnikov is a controversial example that highlights some technical aspects of sustainable design in a memorable way – once the moral factors are disregarded. Since 2011, by the way, there has been a Kalashnikov in the collection of the Design Museum London – as a design classic.

⚠ In our understanding, good design should not be deadly, nor should it kill or induce to kill.

"Make Love, Not War"
was a popular slogan of the U.S. protest movement against the Vietnam War. It is not clear who coined the saying. In the mid-1960s, it spread quickly in the hippie movement as an updated interpretation of "Make Peace, Not War". To date, the iconic slogan can still be found on pins, in fashion or in music.

The Maker's Bill of Rights

The Maker's Bill of Rights is a memorandum calling for the reparability of the products that surround us, published in 2005 in the online magazine *makezine*. This memorandum includes some of the points of sustainable design that we find applied in the Kalashnikov.

Since its release, the manifesto has circulated in the maker community as a course of action for open-source activists and future-oriented, sustainable manufacturers. In its expanded, illustrated form, the basic guidelines can be found – with an introductory emphasis that relates directly to the responsibilities of designers: Ease of repair shall be a design ideal, not an afterthought.

(+) Work against planned obsolescence and pay attention to ease of repair when buying new products – such as whether there are screws on the housing, or spare parts are available. Try to repair your defective products. Use the knowledge of local establishments and (crowd-based/global) exchange platforms on the industry's planned vulnerabilities and be critical of statements made by the manufacturer.

(+) Design products with a modular structure. Avoid parts that wear out. If this is not possible, be sure that they are interchangeable and easily accessible. Indicate where spare parts are available. If your clients require planned obsolescence, refuse and advise them on the need for a new product culture. (A Global Issue ↗)

makezine.com

THE MAKER'S BILL OF RIGHTS

■ Meaningful and specific parts lists shall be included.
■ Cases shall be easy to open. ■ Batteries shall be replaceable. ■ Special tools are allowed only for darn good reasons. ■ Profiting by selling expensive special tools is wrong, and not making special tools available is even worse. ■ Torx is OK; tamperproof is rarely OK.
■ Components, not entire subassemblies, shall be replaceable. ■ Consumables, like fuses and filters, shall be easy to access. ■ Circuit boards shall be commented.
■ Power from USB is good; power from proprietary power adapters is bad. ■ Standard connectors shall have pinouts defined. ■ If it snaps shut, it shall snap open. ■ Screws better than glues. ■ Docs and drivers shall have permalinks and shall reside for all perpetuity at archive.org. ■ Ease of repair shall be a design ideal, not an afterthought. ■ Metric or standard, not both.
■ Schematics shall be included.

Make:
technology on your time

Drafted by Mister Jalopy, with assistance from Phillip Torrone and Simon Hill.

WE HOLD THESE TRUTHS TO BE SELF-EVIDENT

SELF-REPAIR MANIFESTO:

REPAIR IS BETTER THAN RECYCLING.
MAKING OUR THINGS LAST LONGER IS BOTH MORE EFFICIENT AND MORE COST-EFFECTIVE THAN MINING THEM FOR RAW MATERIALS.

REPAIR SAVES THE PLANET.
EARTH HAS LIMITED RESOURCES AND WE CAN'T RUN A LINEAR MANUFACTURING PROCESS FOREVER. THE BEST WAY TO BE EFFICIENT IS TO REUSE WHAT WE ALREADY HAVE!

REPAIR SAVES YOU MONEY.
FIXING THINGS IS OFTEN FREE, AND USUALLY CHEAPER THAN REPLACING THEM. DOING THE REPAIR YOURSELF SAVES SERIOUS DOUGH.

REPAIR TEACHES ENGINEERING.
THE BEST WAY TO FIND OUT HOW SOMETHING WORKS IS TO TAKE IT APART!

IF YOU CAN'T FIX IT, YOU DON'T OWN IT.
REPAIR CONNECTS PEOPLE AND DEVICES, CREATING BONDS THAT TRANSCEND CONSUMPTION. SELF-REPAIR IS SUSTAINABLE.

REPAIR CONNECTS YOU WITH YOUR THINGS ○ REPAIR EMPOWERS AND EMBOLDENS INDIVIDUALS
REPAIR TRANSFORMS CONSUMERS INTO CONTRIBUTORS ○ REPAIR INSPIRES PRIDE IN OWNERSHIP
REPAIR INJECTS SOUL AND MAKES THINGS UNIQUE ○ REPAIR IS INDEPENDENCE
REPAIR REQUIRES CREATIVITY ○ REPAIR IS GREEN ○ REPAIR IS JOYFUL
REPAIR IS NECESSARY FOR UNDERSTANDING OUR THINGS ○ REPAIR SAVES MONEY AND RESOURCES

WE HAVE THE RIGHT:

TO OPEN AND REPAIR OUR THINGS—WITHOUT VOIDING THE WARRANTY ○ TO DEVICES THAT CAN BE OPENED
TO ERROR CODES AND WIRING DIAGRAMS ○ TO TROUBLESHOOTING INSTRUCTIONS AND FLOWCHARTS
TO REPAIR DOCUMENTATION FOR EVERYTHING ○ TO CHOOSE OUR OWN REPAIR TECHNICIAN
TO REMOVE 'DO NOT REMOVE' STICKERS ○ TO REPAIR THINGS IN THE PRIVACY OF OUR OWN HOMES
TO REPLACE ANY AND ALL CONSUMABLES OURSELVES
TO HARDWARE THAT DOESN'T REQUIRE PROPRIETARY TOOLS TO REPAIR
TO AVAILABLE, REASONABLY PRICED SERVICE PARTS

INSPIRED BY MISTER JALOPY'S MAKER'S BILL OF RIGHTS AND PLATFORM 21'S REPAIR MANIFESTO

A symbol of resistance

The fist thrust into the air – a symbolic gesture that goes back to the revolt of the working class against low wages and poor working conditions – here in combination with the wrench is a symbol of the rebellion against the paternalism of industry, which makes the independent repair of products impossible; against the throw-away society and for the self-empowerment of a group of like-minded people in a struggle for the right to repair and in a struggle for quality. In the re-appropriation of a symbol that stands for a social and political movement, a new collective identity is founded. The agents in the repair revolution are globally networked; they stand for a loose, open movement, are rhizomatically structured and act within the meaning of sharing and mutual learning.

An important tool for this is the tutorials or workshops that are published on the Internet in the form of videos, written instructions, blogs or forums. In this way, experts and lay people alike bring their knowledge together to enable what should be self-evident: the maintenance and repair of our stuff.

⚠ Join the Repair Revolution.

8

Tools for the Design Revolution

⑧ Long Life

What it takes to use things over generations

As part of Vienna Design Week 2013, the IDRV researched the existing potential of Vienna's 4th municipal district, which offers residents opportunities to have their things repaired, purchase used items, or even make things. A tour led to the often ignored and perhaps not yet sufficiently used small service providers of an alternative consumption and production culture opposed to the throw-away society. We spoke with the owners of these shops and received important suggestions on how things could be used longer.

(+) This knowledge is learned on the street, not in school or at university.

(+) Existing infrastructure often has untapped potential. Design can help to develop this potential and establish new concepts successfully.

(+) The local infrastructure is a knowledge base and a laboratory for future consumption and production patterns! Let us learn there and use design strategies to transform them into sustainable and multipliable models of a new way of life.

At the doll doctor

The visit to the doll doctor turned into a philosophical analysis of the current state of our consumer culture. Most cheap, disposable toys, as those that are sold everywhere today, do not end up in the repair shop, but in the trash. They do not cost very much, and can therefore be bought mindlessly on a shopping impulse. The dolls that look out from the doll doctor's crowded shelves come from another time. An era in which people saved a long time for a doll. And a time when an emotional attachment to the doll was formed that spanned its entire anticipated useful life – childhood – and beyond. The construction of the old jointed dolls made them easily repairable. The rubber cords that hold the limbs together – and forgive the malpositions of the doll – can easily be replaced whenever there is a torn ligament. In several drawers, the doll doctor has the components of a classic jointed doll that can break or wear out in stock as spare parts: hands, arms, feet, hair and eyes. The doll companies used to deliver replacement parts. They don't anymore. Reparability is no longer the highest design principle; instead, it is the predetermined breaking point.

Just a few years ago, anyone who wanted to remove the head of a famous American doll could do so and put it back again. Today, this funny game means a broken doll's neck. A small part in the neck breaks, and the head is separate from the doll from now on. These are the product innovations of industry today.

(+) The doll, as it used to be made, is a metaphor for a category of future objects. It represents the objects for which we still keep a strong emotional connection and treat with respect even after active use.

(+) The doll doctor can be seen as a model for a local repair infrastructure. He holds the connection to the centralized production units of a new culture of objects.

The furniture restorer
If you want to know how to design the most durable furniture possible, a furniture restoration workshop is the place where this knowledge is conveyed in a credible and exciting way. Cheap furniture very seldom ends up here. Often there are antiques or design classics from the recent past. A broken Ant chair by Arne Jacobsen can be found there as well as a historicist cabinet that is more than a hundred years old. Cultural appreciation, family history or just good workmanship has saved this furniture from the waste incineration plant – the modern crematorium for the things of the throw-away society. For example, the famous "Viennese wickerwork" – the woven rattan of bentwood chairs – often needs repairing. After all, this natural material can still be found today, and customized with the same artisanship as it once was for the chairs. The restorer told us about thick wood veneers that are treated so that, in most cases, the old protective layer can be removed and reapplied without removing any material; about surfaces that become more and more beautiful with use and take on a patina. Who in the design process today is already thinking about how an object will look in a hundred years with patina?

The furniture restorer even has a tip for furniture made of pressed particleboard that is frequently assembled and disassembled: simply put a match in the loose screw hole, and then tighten the screw. Such furniture is not usually restored – but perhaps in the distant future ...

(+) A beautiful patina is a protective coating for durability. Surfaces should be designed so that they not only age gracefully, but can also be renewed inexpensively over and over.

Italian espresso and racing bikes
There is a shop that seems to come from a time when dirty bicycle chains and the best espresso were not a contradiction – a symbiosis that has its prototype in Italy. The shop sells both coffee and vintage bikes with frames made of steel. This is very durable and will not break after a few years – like frames made from aluminum.

The historic wheels are elegant and, in urban areas today, they have become fetishes of a new mobility culture. Since the bicycle components were also available independent from the producers (and they still are), reparability is guaranteed long after the end of the respective bicycle producers. In Vienna, however, there is only one master who learned the bicycle repair trade – a knowledge loss for sustainable mobility in the future!

(+) Think of things that are configurable from finished components. This ensures a long reparability without altering the aesthetics. Later, however, deliberate technological adaptations can be made.

(+) Simple materials often guarantee a longer lifespan than technologically superior materials. In addition, local repair options are easier to provide if no difficult procedures (such as aluminum welding) are used.

(+) In order to make used things attractive to new groups of buyers, other contextualizations are needed.

The violin as a model

For us, the violin is a symbol of a category of objects that can last for centuries and still be in use every day. If we want to design sustainable things, we can learn from the violin. After a long development and cultural variations, the musical instrument found a final form, which became common practice ever since. The violin experienced its proliferation in a time when patent rights had not yet been invented. Reverse engineering or copying was not a criminal offense, but an appreciation of the extraordinary achievements of the pioneers of the art of violin making.

Reparability

Although at first glance violins do not look like "design for reparability", they can be repaired and maintained very well. With a thin knife, you can pry between the rib and the reinforced edge of the violin and remove either the top or the bottom. A glue whose simple composition is known to every luthier worldwide ensures the stable conjoining of all parts and, at the same time, allows easy disassembly. The edge of the violin is designed so that the knife can be used without damaging the lateral surfaces; at the same time, it is also a decorative element.

Replacement parts

The luthier does not have the necessary spare parts lying finished in a drawer. However, only the raw material of wood is required to produce them. Therefore it is possible, at any time and any place, to manufacture a part immediately through local production and use it to replace a defective part.

The magic of things

Violins become more valuable through their proper use by outstanding artists. They gain a distinctive story that inscribes itself into the object. In an animistic way, we still believe in a simple law of magic – namely, that things retain a connection with the people who have touched them.

Cooperation

We were also inspired by the accounts of meetings between luthiers, where they regularly share their experiences and discuss the impact of new technologies on the art of violin making. The knowledge of violin making is transmitted from one generation to the next, as has been customary in the trade for centuries. That the luthier we visited is also a musician and gives lessons in his workshop showed us an alternative form of a production site, which is used at the same time for the transfer of knowledge.

(+) The luthier's workshop is a metaphor for a future production site. The values and strategies we appreciate are certainly applicable to new forms of local production and repair infrastructure.

(+) The design of the future can be measured against the idea of the violin.

(+) The local production of spare parts, or at least their availability, allows a long lifespan for things that need repair. New technologies (such as FabLab = Fabrication Laboratory) can ensure the availability of complex parts in the future. As a result, new product concepts that can be used for a long time are realizable.

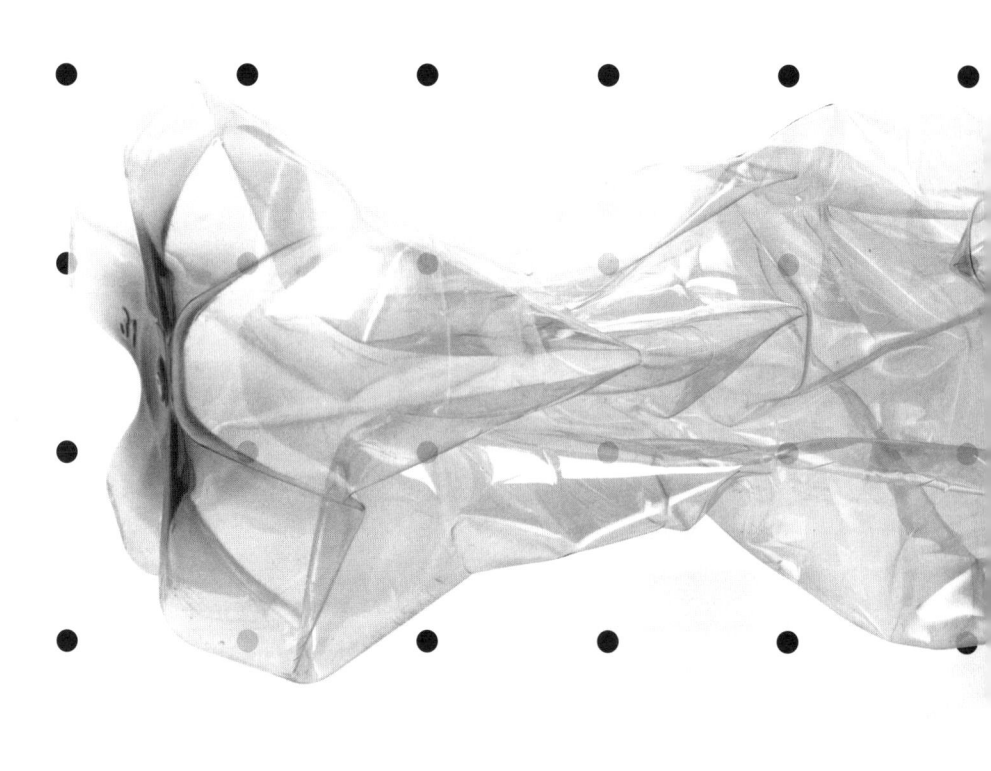

9

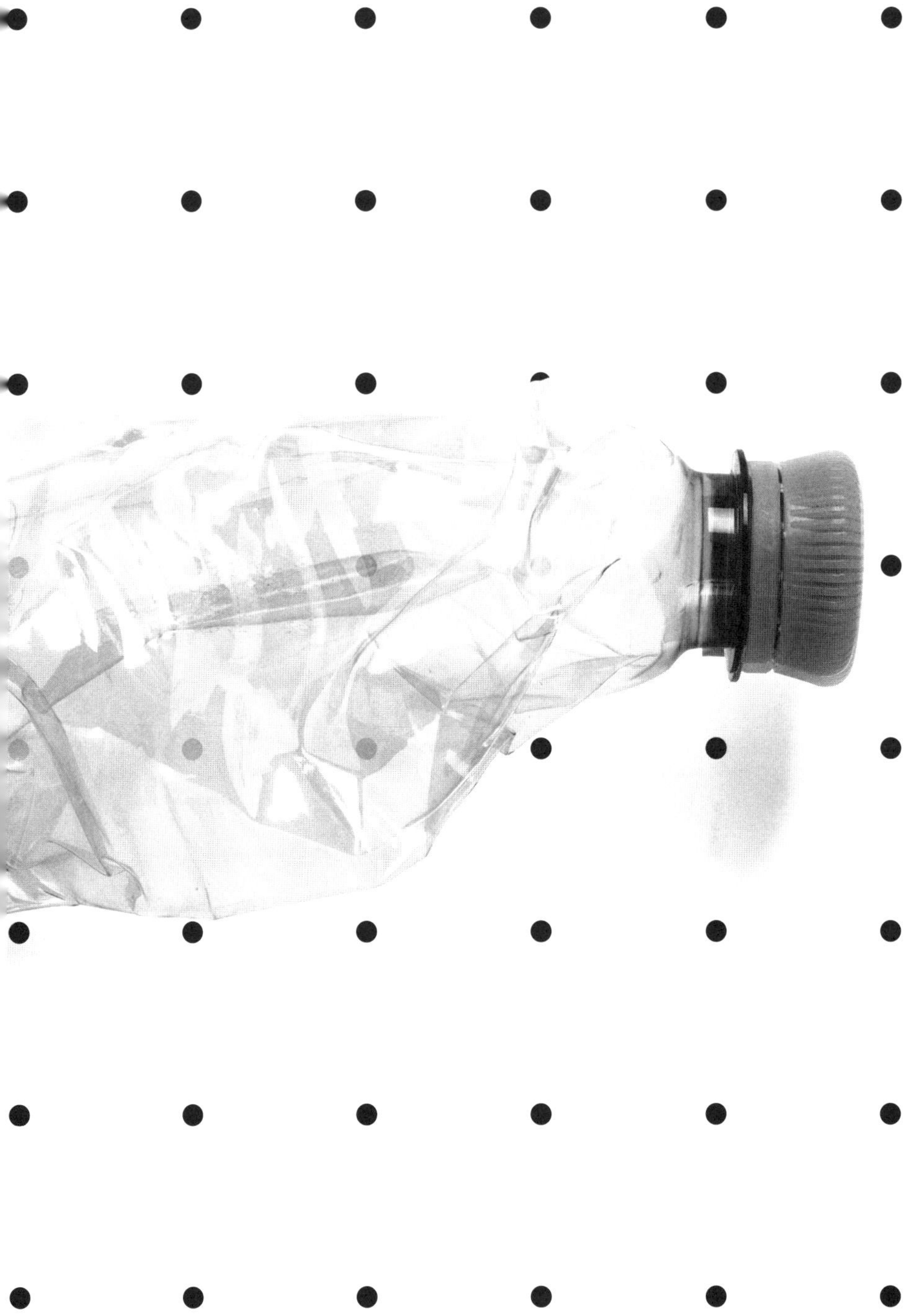

⑨ Resurrection

The cycles of nature inspire and influence our perceptions. This gives rise to religious thoughts as well as technological progress.

The cycle of nature – its constant renewal – is an essential part of the grand narratives of humanity. The return of spring was the most important time of year in many agrarian societies. In different forms, following his ritual death, the grain god experiences resurrection and a new life. So too did nature awaken in the minds of our ancestors every year from its slumber. Today, in our consumer society, consumption has taken on a religious character, and thus new myths and rituals of immortality re-emerge – in the form of products that are brought out every year under the same name as new.

Biological cycles
Using the sun, plants can produce organic substances from inorganic substances. These plants then become food for other creatures, which serve again as food for others, and so on. The dead organic matter from plants and animals is broken down by organisms back to inorganic materials; this is the biological cycle. Large biological cycles are called ecological cycles. The human way of life has disrupted this natural metabolism. The biocapacity provided by nature has been increasingly strained since industrialization. Our lifestyle, especially in the industrialized countries, is causing more and more damage to the air, water, soil, and of course also to humans. The exact extent of these harmful influences can be calculated. (Life Cycle Analysis ↗)

Solar energy
The sun's energy is free – yet still people are not able to meet their energy needs sufficiently through renewable energy sources. We need to break our addiction to fossil fuels in the coming decades. An important step towards a sustainable future is the conversion of energy production to renewable energy sources. Nature demonstrates how incredible things can be made out of a little solar energy. We need to learn from this.

Natural cycle

How can things be produced that are part of the biological cycle? William McDonough and Michael Braungart have popularized cyclical thinking with their book *Cradle to Cradle. Remaking the Way We Make Things* (2002). But this idea, so important to society, became a business, and the established keyword "Cradle to Cradle (C2C)" became a trademark. The fewest certified products receive the Platinum award – the most stringent category – although even this category doesn't require what will be urgently needed in the future. These are the criteria for basic certification:

- Identification of all ingredients
- Allocation of substances into biological or technological cycles
- Are the materials harmless to humans and the environment?
- A strategy on how to deal with ingredients that are still problematic
- A plan on how a biological or technological cycle can be established
- How is the necessary energy produced?

These are all important questions that companies should be asking themselves. But there is nothing here about a cycle; at most, it is on the level of strategies and intentions. The platinum category actually requests more learning from nature – a shame that even committed companies can hardly reach it:

- No problematic substances that endanger humans or the environment
- Establishment of a collection system for used products
- An equivalent or an even better product can be produced out of the existing product
- At least an eighty percent recycling rate for the ingredients
- Use of fifty percent of solar energy for the entire product (not just in production!)
- Active water conservation
- Independently certified corporate social responsibility

Tools for the Design Revolution

A T-shirt like a leaf?

How does a T-shirt need to be made in order to fit into a natural cycle? It needs to be made from natural materials, such as cotton. According to the Water Footprint Network, a global average of 10,000 liters of water is needed for irrigation in the production of one kilogram of cotton. This comes to about 2,500 liters per T-shirt. In some parts of the world, large amounts of water are not available without environmental damage and social injustice. Then the fibers must be dyed – and here, unfortunately, even today additional substances are used that are dangerous to humans and the environment. They have no place in biological cycles. A sustainable product should not only be less harmful to the environment; it should have a positive impact – it should even be nourishment.

On the compost heap
We took a T-shirt that matches the criteria of a natural cycle in some respects (C2C) and buried it in a compost pile. After a few weeks, the garment begins to decompose. Since the coloring is non-toxic, the resulting earth can safely be used for the cultivation of food or even cotton once more. Sounds good, doesn't it? It would, if it were not for the problem of the closed cycle. The establishment of closed nutrient cycles is a major challenge for many of the products that we use. And finally, not everyone has a compost heap. If, on the other hand, we were to throw the shirt into the organic waste, it would be fished out again in the sorting for composting.

Tools for the Design Revolution   129

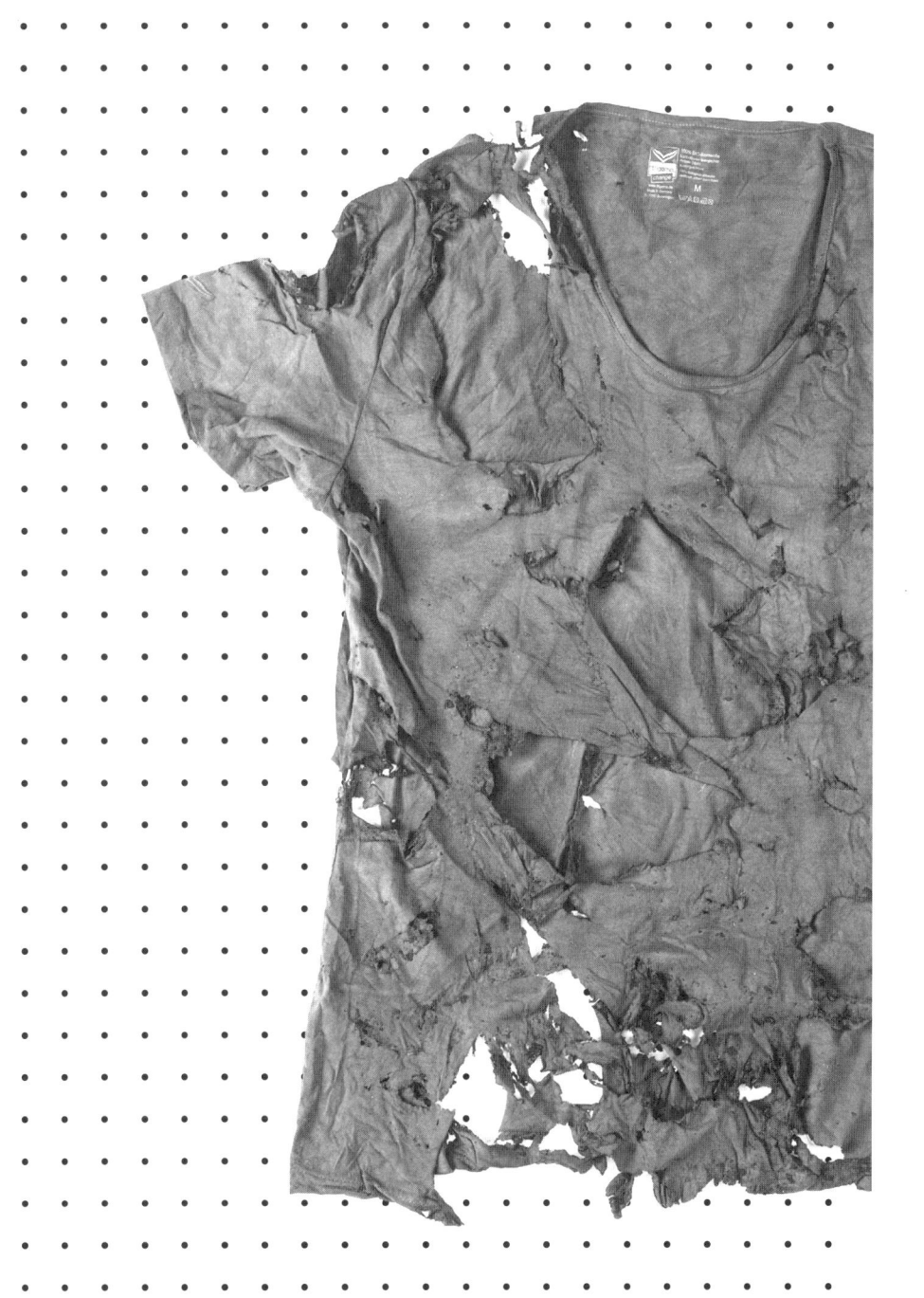

Industrial composting
The composting method currently used for organic plant waste, for example, is not applicable for garments. A separate process and collection system would have to be set up for clothing or packing materials. In the best case, other products could also be recycled in the same way. This is a challenge for the future, however, which would only fail today, in no small part because ecological action is financially unattractive due to the lack of environmental cost transparency. Today, the refuse incinerator gets an attractive disposal fee for a garment, and may even produce some energy through its combustion. Prices would have to be determined by the environmental consequences of the products; then the more dangerous products would be much more expensive.

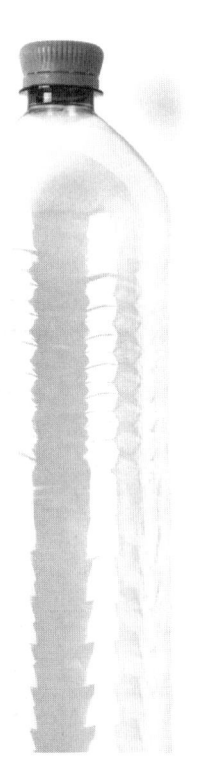

⚠ Consumers should critically question the "compostable" designation on products: Are they really being composted? Can they be disposed of in the existing collection systems? The purchase of products ideally supports an important process that will hopefully lead in the future to the establishment of products in biological product cycles.

⊕ Design for all life cycle phases: Has the product's return to the biological cycle been ensured? The creation of collection systems and the practicality and feasibility of composting is just as important as the design of the product itself!

⊕ Companies can also establish product criteria for biological cycles without certification, therefore demonstrating corporate social responsibility.

Technical cycle
Inspired by nature, humans have also created technological cycles. There are materials that, if correctly collected and sorted, can be used again as raw material for the same products. But the recycling of these materials is not very attractive for the raw material extraction industry. Therefore, new material properties are always invented that hinder a cyclical economy without quality loss. After all, more should always be sold, not less. Nature, however, is able to generate highly diversified properties in the same biological cycles. We need to learn from this.

Recycling
Separating the trash usually fills us with a sufficiently good conscience. It shouldn't. Only when things are made from one hundred percent recycled materials, becoming new source material without any loss of quality whatsoever, using energy that is derived entirely from renewable sources – only then can we sit back and relax. But this is not the case in the foreseeable future. Waste piles are transported by trucks across continents or sent overseas. Global production is followed by the global disposal of our mountains of waste.

"We have therefore tried to point out in the advertising of some of our European customers how enjoyable it really is to throw things away. This is an almost anti-materialist stance."

Ernest Dichter, 1971 (1985:238)

The pioneer of commercial motivation research, Ernest Dichter, here encapsulates the strategy of the consumption industry in the early 1970s: After a period of market saturation, it took a throwaway culture to keep the market stimulated. Whoever would not follow the dictates of disposability would be socially ostracized. And those who were good consumers were encouraged to own multiple items of the same type. But we are none the wiser; we still follow the dictates of the throw-away society willingly.

Loss of material
Not everything that can be recycled is collected. Therefore, large material losses are already being caused by the unwillingness of consumers to use the existing collection systems. This is made worse by the fact that recycling processes cannot recover one hundred percent of the material; they also often need energy and a lot of water or chemicals. Let us not be blinded by the recycling symbol on products and packaging. The arrows pointing in a circle suggest an endless cycle, but the reality seems to be different.

⚠ Reduce/ Reuse/ Recover – this well-known formula should be applied in the correct order. Only if reuse is not possible should material be recycled. Particularly in the packaging industry, where materials are only used briefly, a huge waste of materials is taking place!

⚠ Recycling rates are often difficult to improve on the technical side because of the processes used. With better-designed services leading to higher collection rates, the proportion of recovered material would be higher. Recycling is an integral part of the design task!

⚠ Electronic products contain hundreds of different materials in small quantities. Recycling processes can scarcely recover these small quantities – so valuable substances are lost.

⊕ Do your own research: A visit to the dump or to the recycler opened our eyes to the reality of the problem of waste.

⊕ Only use materials that can be recycled without a loss of quality.

⊕ Check the processes by which products are recycled. Can the materials be separated and sorted? What really happens during recycling?

10

Eco-Shape

BIO*LINE*

go green

✓ FAIR

Blue Power

CO2

eco
Logo

CERTIFIED PRODUCT
100% BIO
FAIR & NATURAL

EcoStyle

Tools for the Design Revolution

⑩ Greenwashing

Tools for
the logo jungle

The increasing attention being paid to the subject of "sustainability" has meant that companies, products, or the ideas of advertising and communications departments are increasingly supplied with apparent and actual attributes to highlight their environmental impact. In this context, there is often only the unfounded production of a seemingly green image; this phenomenon is called greenwashing. This does not always happen in order to deliberately mislead. Often, what is behind it is a pure lack of information on established standards. Sometimes these communication activities border on negligence, such as when an oil company loudly puts a minimal fraction of its investments into alternative energy, and decorates its logo with pretty, abstract green leaves, but on the whole, it clings to the exploitation of finite resources and colonialist practices. In such cases, the implausible focus of the company will quickly be revealed. It becomes difficult when logos or certificates are invented, when concepts are exhausted by their inflationary application, half-truths are spread, or system limits are set so that the result consistently looks good.

Words

Greenwashing happens in words and images, or in the combination of the two. Terms like bio, biological, organic, natural or sustainable are now used in such an inflationary way that their original meanings have partially shifted. "Clean coal" and "environmentally friendly CO_2 emissions" sound like heavenly solutions to all our energy needs. Biodiesel seems like it should be as environmentally friendly as food – but what gets concealed is the fact that, in addition to other disadvantages, land for the production of biodiesel is currently in competition with land for food production. Being CO_2 neutral sounds pretty liberating, but it does not necessarily mean that no CO_2 is released – rather that this is only being compensated through neutralization whenever possible. When, for example, CO_2 neutrality of an industrialized country is achieved mainly through emissions trading, but no emissions are really being saved, something is not right.

The power of words is found in the associations they arouse in us, and so now I can apparently fly without emitting CO_2 or be CO_2-neutral when I send mail.

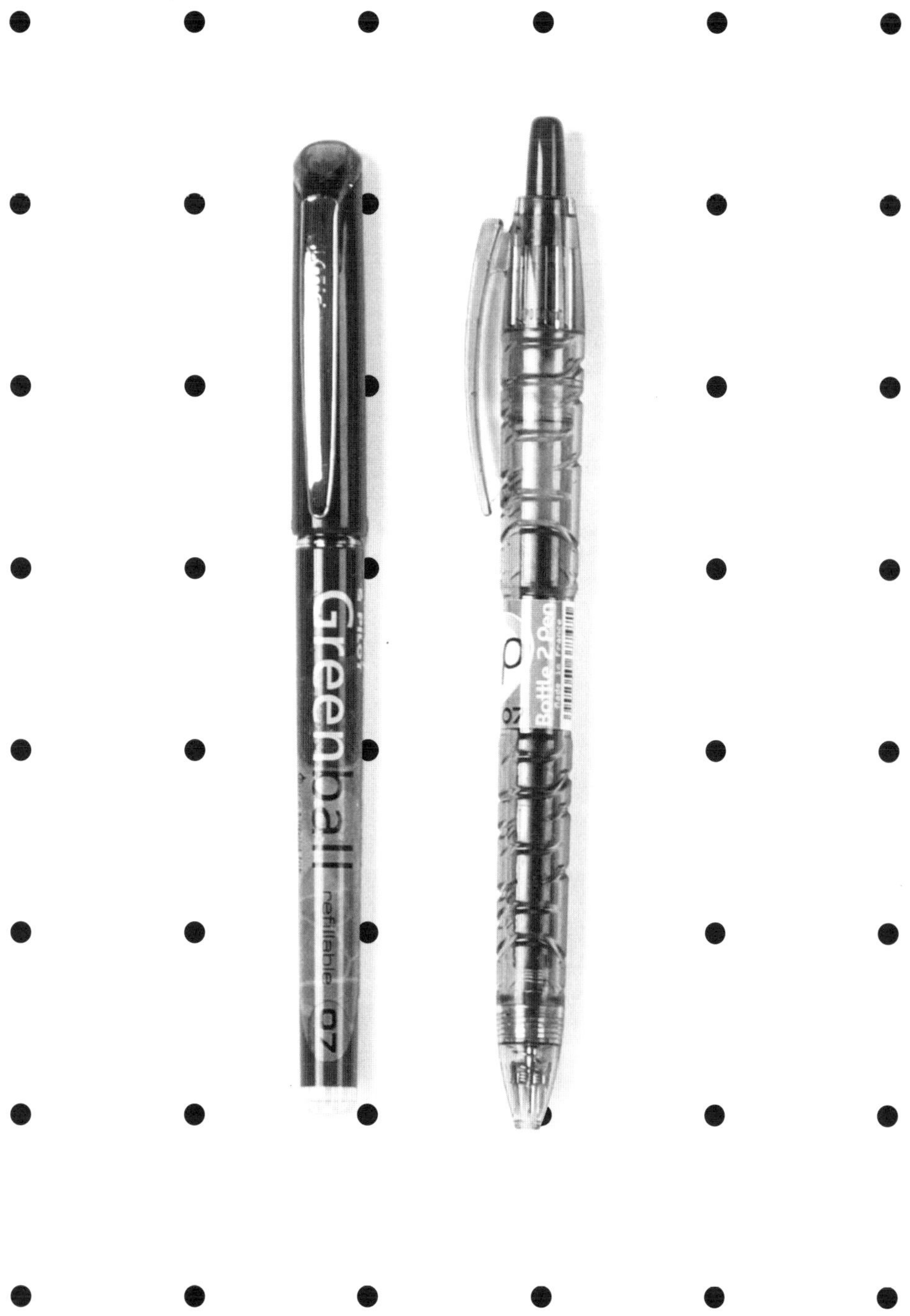
PILOT
Greenball
refillable
07
Bottle 2 Pen
07

Images

On the visual level of greenwashing, the paint can is often used to make an image tangible; blue and green are the favorite colors – so pure, so clean, so natural. Consulting firms or advertising departments often use the broadest possible brush. A green-colored font makes the word "environmentally friendly" even more environmentally friendly. Leaves, trees or raindrops are probably the most frequently used images from nature that suggest that we are dealing with an eco-friendly product. The shimmering blue ballpoint pens whose bodies resemble plastic bottles tell their own story of recycling – they are the descendants of recycled PET bottles and bring to mind fresh, clear water. The silhouette of a car hovers over the term "environmentally rated", and already we think this rating is valuable, whether or not it is certified, or actually environmentally friendly – that's in the eye of the beholder. The imagination knows no limits here. But there are limits to trust – in what is presented to us every day. We shouldn't put up with it any longer!

(+) The discourse on sustainability in general likes to use religious scenarios or principles such as the Ten Commandments. Therefore it is not surprising that the practice of greenwashing was classified into the *Seven Sins of Greenwashing* by the TerraChoice environmental agency.

⚠ It should be asked why sustainable strategies are labeled, and those products and concepts that are harmful are not given warning signs.

140 Tools for the Design Revolution

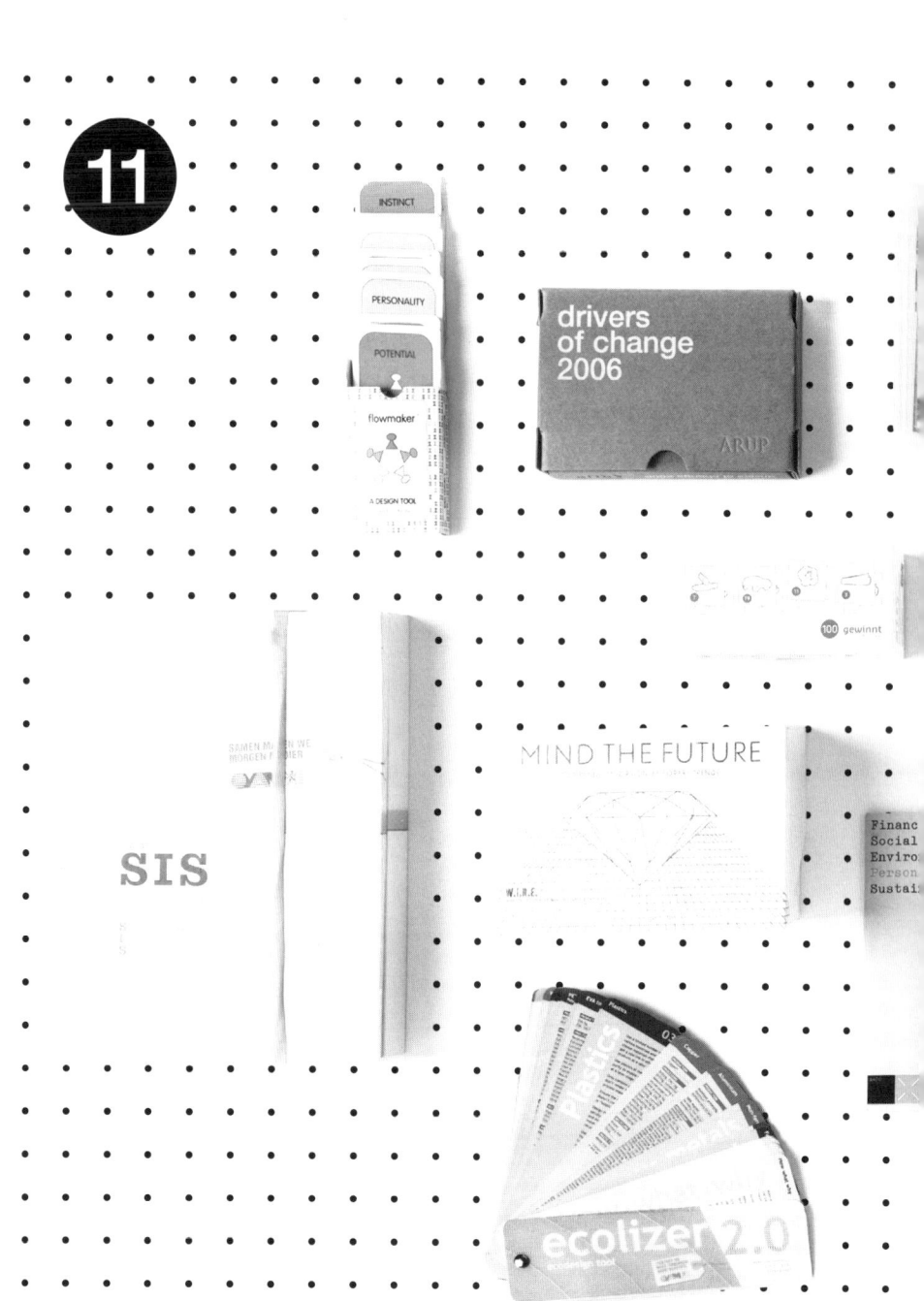

DESIGN TOOL

Tools for the Design Revolution 141

⑪ Creativity Tools

Think of the world playfully

Sustainable design matrix

sustainability potential

eco-centric approach

transition scenario
(doing things less)

idea of well-being
(access-based well-being)

status of goods
(shared & common goods)

type of innovation
(behavioral innovation)

designing new production consumption systems

creating new scenarios

system approach

transition scenario
(doing things less & better)

idea of well-being
(context-based well-being)

status of goods
(shared & common goods)

type of innovation
(system innovation)

transition scenario (n/a)

idea of well-being
(product-based well-being)

status of goods
(owned & remedial goods)

type of innovation (n/a)

status quo

redesign of existing products & services

designing new products & services

transition scenario (n/a)

idea of well-being
(product-based well-being)

status of goods
(owned & remedial goods)

type of innovation (n/a)

techno-centric approach

status quo

Source: Bernhard Dusch, 2013; based on Konrad et al. (2003) and Vezzoli / Manzini (2008)

142 Tools for the Design Revolution

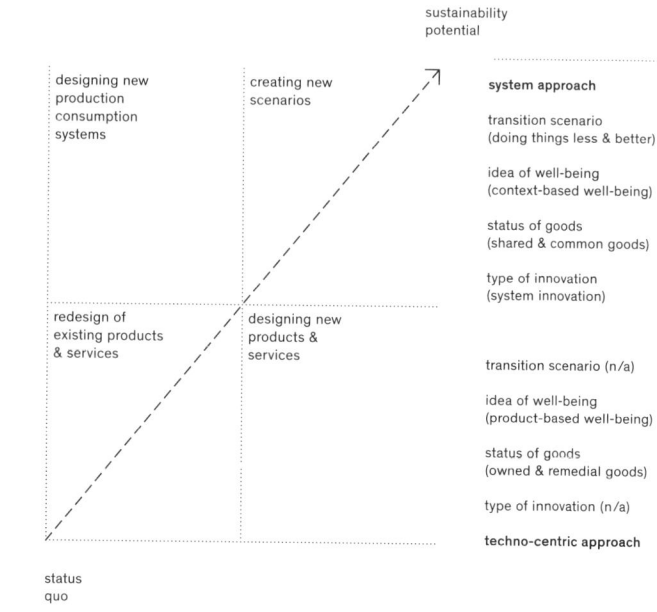

There are a variety of methods for generating ideas – not only in the design field. Brainstorming, storytelling and mind maps are useful tools to communicate and sort through the ideas that are bouncing around. Using mood boards and personas, for example, products can be positioned so that they appeal to a defined group of consumers or awaken their desires. In practice, this often leads to products that we do not necessarily need, whose designs, combined with clever marketing strategies, produce a constant demand for the latest trends. On the other hand, this knowledge can also be used in conjunction with methodical design to establish measures for a sustainable world.

Where to?
The "One Tonne Life" example (World Calculation Models ↗) has shown that any objectives that arise from the world calculation models cannot be achieved sufficiently through technical innovation alone. Rather, we must also change our behavior.

To define a target for the design process or to situate the status quo, matrices that reflect the different directions of development are useful. The Sustainable Design Matrix from the Cambridge Sustainable Design Toolkit, for example, places technical innovation on its horizontal axis and the innovation potential of a change in behavior on the vertical. Redesigns of conventional products that have been improved ecologically in some way are located in the lower ranges, while measures that motivate users to change their habits can be found in the upper ranges. With the combination of technical innovation and a change of user behavior, the potential for innovation increases in favor of sustainable development.

(+) Take advantage of the variety of design possibilities! The new behaviors of people are just as malleable as technical features. Other usage patterns demand radically new products – or dematerialize them.

⚠ Only through the integration of sustainable design knowledge at the beginning of a product or system development process can it be ensured that the objectives of sustainable development will be pursued. Cosmetic procedures are only a course correction and tend to miss the mark.

But how?

Guides, roadmaps, do's and don'ts, criteria lists, commandments, and even common sense point the way to decisions that are designed for the future. The number of criteria lists – partially rooted in the manifestos of companies and design studios – is huge, but these well-intentioned resolutions so far do not seem to come true in their application. But the criteria indicate the right direction and are helpful in scrutinizing and evaluating concepts. They also enable the assessment of the social and abstract requirements that cannot be mapped only according to their environmental impact.

⚠ Ask the right questions, or: "Trust is good, control is better". The existence of ecologically and socially sustainable business principles does not mean that they are well established at all levels. Only if you are curious and question things skeptically can you find out what materials are really put into the products and vendor parts, what the working conditions are like, what waste is produced and how the well-intentioned energy efficiency program is really applied.

Search for alternatives

Not all of the routes that have already been embarked upon are sustainable. At the same time, strategic tools for the future help to design frameworks and other forms of coexistence or to generate lifestyles under changed conditions. In this way, the looming problems of the future are addressed or the parameters of the new lifestyles are accepted as a starting point.

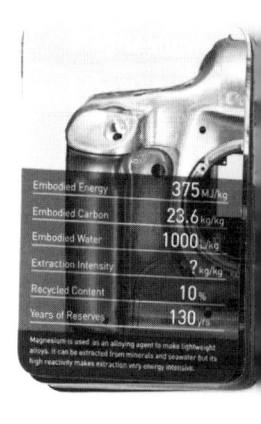

⊕ Scenario cards help when looking into the future. Immanent problems inspire solutions that help to design a better future; new fields of activity are opening up. Expertise is not always needed to generate alternatives.

⚠ (Future Concepts ↗)

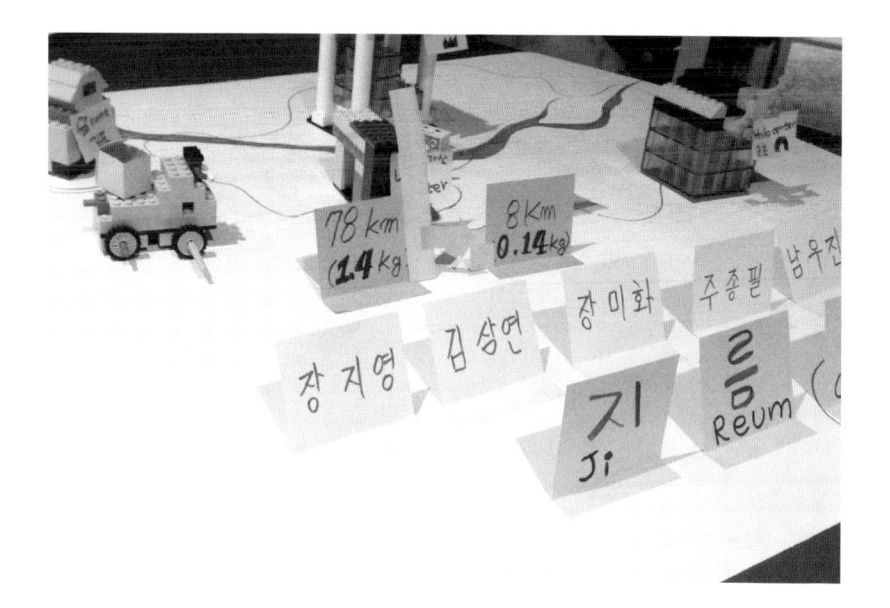

Just a couple of figures

Juggling tables and figures does not describe the everyday situation of design today. However, numbers are necessary to make informed decisions on environmental impacts. With the help of decks of cards, apps and other prepared figures, which provide information on the environmental impact of different materials, scenarios and designs can be compared playfully and the best material in each respective impact category can be found during the design process – almost like a card game.

⚠ The figures in the decks of cards do not usually illuminate all environmental impacts and only relate to one material or one phase of the product life cycle. They are practical for everyday design, but do not replace the more holistic view permitted by a life cycle assessment.

⚠ Apps can be helpful, but they should not encourage us to switch off our self-reliant thinking or neutralize the autonomy of the subject.

Create scenarios

The observation, consideration and design of product-service concepts and the entire life cycle can be very abstract. With the help of scenario tools, concepts can be visualized and compared. In this way, various resources can be used to support the testing of the theoretical concepts.

(+) Building blocks are ideally suited to test product-service concepts playfully in interdisciplinary teams.

Is that so?

Mood boards or personas can be used to check whether concepts have to be adapted to the needs of specific groups so that they will accept, for example, a change in user behavior at all. Through user interviews or ergonomic analysis, the feelings of the user can be determined and verified.

⚠ Only when the well-being of the users is guaranteed will new services be accepted. Particularly in concepts of using instead of owning, it is a great challenge to make the benefits and the quality of the sharing economy tangible, and thus to provide a real alternative to ownership.

⊕ Numbers can annoy, but they can also encourage creativity. Living in the future with only one ton of CO_2 is a game that generates many new solutions.

Observe the signs

There is no single roadmap to sustainable design solutions. The creativity tools can open up new possibilities, but only in combination with design knowledge for the future. Calls for improvements and savings made with a wagging finger will only partially succeed. Instead, positive experiences need to be created – this applies in the design process just as in the use of alternatives. Here, too, the world issue and the calculation models serve as limiting factors.

⚠ The use of creativity tools in a team from various disciplines reduces the danger of thinking in only one direction and increases the number of potential alternatives. They are useful in overcoming outdated/ossified structures and in sharing the existing knowledge of individuals.

⊕ Use free tools! It is not always necessary to buy a tool or to book a training seminar. Often it is sufficient to use a recent newspaper essay or the evaluation criteria of an eco-design prize to think about the future.

12

Tools for the Design Revolution   149

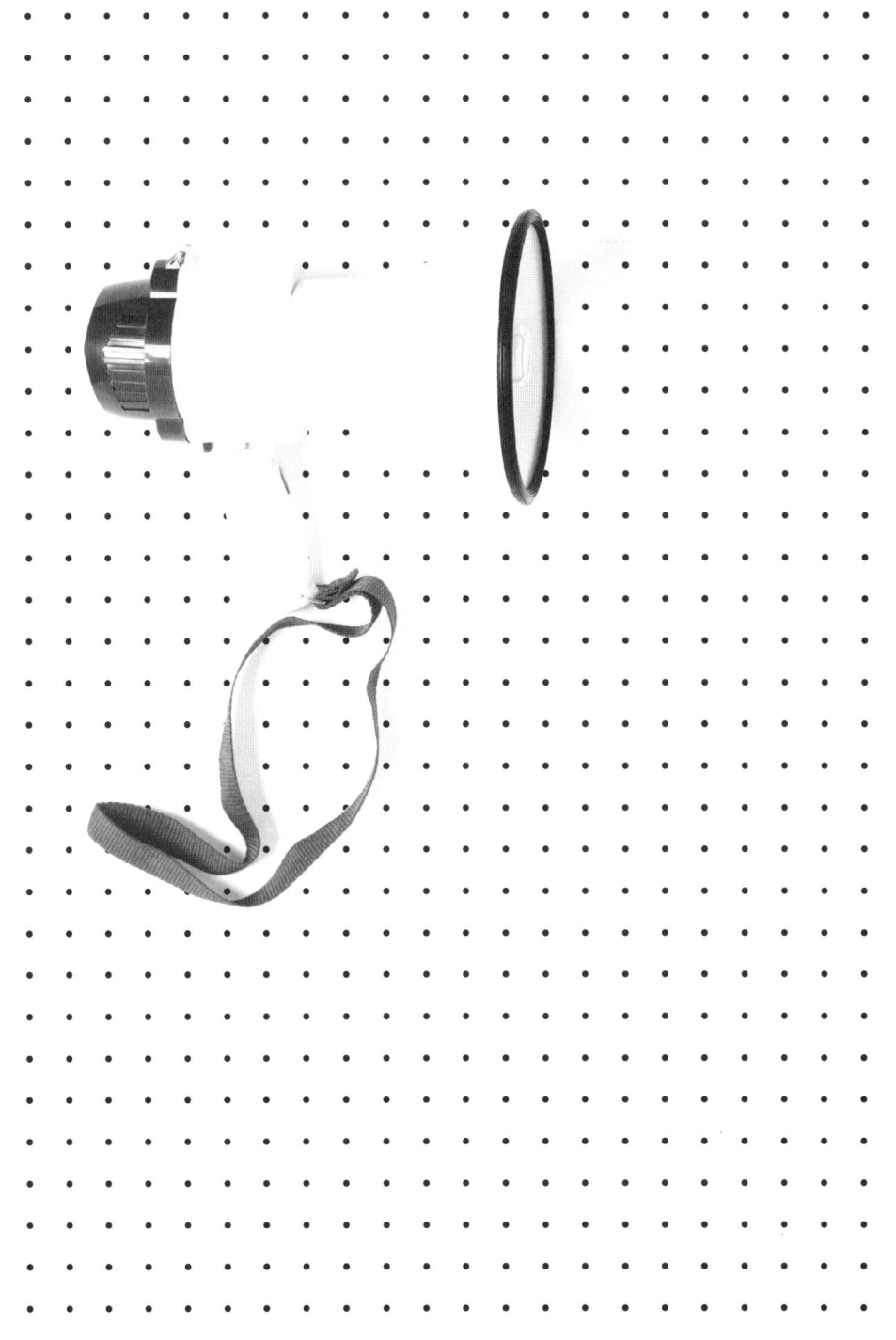

⑫ Offending the Audience

From Design Theory
and Practice.

"You chuckle-heads,
you small-timers,
you nervous nellies,
you fuddy-duddies,
you windbags,
you sitting ducks,
you milquetoasts."

Peter Handke, 1966 (2012:15)

You expected something.
Maybe you expected something else.
You expected objects.
You expected no objects.
You expected an atmosphere.
You expected another world.
You expected no other world.
At best, you expected what you're hearing now.
But even in this case, you expected something else.

You have become a dangerous breed.

There are professions more harmful than industrial design, but only very few of them. And possibly only one profession is phonier: advertising design. You persuade people to buy things they do not need, with money they do not have to impress people who do not care …

You design nonsensical things that are sold by the millions.

Before, if you liked killing people, you had to become general, purchase a coalmine or else study nuclear physics. Today, you have put murder on a mass production basis. By designing criminally unsafe automobiles, by creating a whole new species of permanent garbage to clutter up the landscape, and by choosing materials and processes that pollute the air.

You have no understanding of the social and moral responsibility of design. You do not understand people and do not have any insight into design processes for the public. You do not understand how to use design as a tool to design for the environment and society. (Papanek)

Look in all directions, not just in one. Housing will be a service, like the telephone service (Fuller). Only the circumstances prevent you from living in them: Someone is already there. You must learn to want silence. You are not able to let go of the sentence, "This is mine". Advertisements are all good; the news is all bad (McLuhan). But how do you experience bad news – it changes you: You are pleased that unemployment is rising. Soon, all that will be required of you will be one hour's work a year (Fuller). What is the function of art? Is it the same for things? You say there are thousands working in art, and only one percent understands what it's really about. Society is changing. Important information is difficult to come by, but soon it will be everywhere. You don't notice it.

For you, design can no longer mean producing more and more objects. You do not challenge the paradigm of the practice of design and the possibilities of industrial production. Eco-design has challenged the paradigms of design and industrial production. You took them for granted and did not question them. You will be a witness to a transitional period in which the traditional value system can no longer cope with the new reality.

You must make your contribution to overcoming technological dependency. Imports must be substituted in order to relieve the critical balance of trade; currency must be saved. You design products with a high use value and a relatively low exchange value. You take advantage of the industrial capacity rationally in order to increase productivity. You standardize components and groups of products and production systems in order to simplify production, reduce costs and achieve technical improvements. You streamline the range of products. You create new approaches to your own material culture. You focus your design work on the following seven problem areas: agriculture, consumer goods, medicine and healthcare, light industry, building components, transportation and industrial and consumer packaging.

You design without acting. Acting without design would be a game. Designing without action is utopia. Your goal is not immediate implementation. You run forward. You have taken the ambiguous task upon yourself to write a history of the future – to describe a world that has not yet been discovered. You are trapped in this utopia, but at the same time, it serves as your springboard. I can talk to you because, despite all the vagueness and indecision, your fundamental instinct is still hope. This does not mean that our hopes must necessarily be the same, however. On the contrary, sometimes it's better that they're not.

You are liberated from the responsibility of being a supplier of ideas. You make sure that, with new tools, everything stays the same. You finally recognize that things with a high symbolic value and a low amount of invention are not the subject of design. You imagine the world as a world of objects and divide it into – for example – houses, streets, traffic lights, kiosks; into coffeemakers, sinks, dishes, table linens. This classification has consequences: it leads to a conception of design with a goal of building a better or a more beautiful coffeemaker – that is, to do what has been recognized as "Gute Form" since the 1950s. You do not recognize the social function of design. You make conventional designs. For the design of tomorrow, you have to be able to design entire invisible systems consisting of objects and interpersonal relationships. You have to make "invisible design".

You are only interested in stimulating mass consumption. Everything made by mass production contributes to pollution and the greenhouse effect. All the "cheap" goods that we have pounded out have proven to be too expensive culturally, socially and environmentally – they are even killing us. The desire to live differently is motivated by self-preservation, and calls for a rapid course change in the way we handle production and consumption.

You are proud that you have helped in the process of designing better products that meet the needs of people and make technology human. Today, we have better houses in which living and working is more comfortable. We have innovative media that keep us informed and entertained in a way we had never dreamed of before. But you have also helped us to keep Pandora's box in our hands – with unimaginable problems that, over the long term, are destroying our culture, our economy and our environment.

When standing, you can be a better heckler. According to human anatomy, heckling can be stronger when standing up. You can clench your fists better. You can show your contrariness. You have greater freedom of movement. You should be less restrained.

This text is a collage of direct and indirect quotations and fragments. The sources are listed in the references.
(References ↗)

Stop waiting, and expect nothing. Do something.

13

We are all des now.

John Thackara, 2005:226

⓭ A Personal Matter

What we can do for a positive future

We know that the world only has a limited biocapacity, that the ecological footprint of the developed countries is far too large and urgently needs to be reduced through binding goals. A life of prosperity for all is completely feasible with today's well-known and global solidarity-based target values of one ton of CO_2-eq per person per year and the energy restrictions of the 2,000-watt society. How? Unfortunately, still too few designers know – or they know, but they don't act accordingly. Making these abstract concepts conceivable and an environmentally compatible and sustainable life preferable today – before more disasters happen – requires design. Designers have the skills and the resources to present alternative living concepts and to make them conceivable and tangible so that a larger number of people perceive them to be a preferable alternative for living today. The digital revolution enables participation, discussion, and ultimately, the financing and production of new approaches in design – without the influence of the existing system of production.

(+) Take informed and decisive action!

(+) Be loud and obstinate! The Design Revolution needs resolute allies. Knowledge of world-compatible strategies is a future resource that is already valuable.

(+) Today, alternative design ideas can be financed and produced successfully without industry. Through new media, they have a broad reach and can catalyze new projects.

(+) Equitable, experimental projects in collaboration with industry are a first step in the right direction and enable mutual learning for the future. This way, new modes of action and strategies can be tested within a limited framework and later transferred to a larger context.

(+) Redefine learning. The newest scientific research is just as important as existing everyday knowledge.

Design for change

An eighty percent reduction in CO_2 emissions in developed countries and a radical reduction of energy consumption in the coming decades will require a complete rethinking of our living environments. Design will go from a cultural force to a catalyst for positive change. The emotional qualities of design must be substantiated by world compatibility. Without responsible action for our own and future generations, design can no longer be conceivable. Our life needs to be redesigned from scratch: The education system, our concept of work and social coexistence, the areas of consumption, housing, mobility and food and everything else that contributes to what we call "prosperity". An appreciation of cultural variety has always been and will continue to be an important driver of diversity and cultural resilience in the future. The development and the rise of the global South is a valuable asset, but also a challenge. This new equilibrium will end the cultural dominance of the global North. Design – understood as a social and cultural discipline – must make a contribution to positive change in the world. Design needs a new role. From a successful service provider to industry, it must evolve to serve society.

Design ensures that participation in the social life of the future will not be characterized by wasteful and destructive consumption. This is a historic opportunity, but also an unprecedented challenge. While in the past, social, cultural or technological reasons have often been the starting point for transformation and change, now it is the insight into the limitations and fragility of the world. This insight will also change design and shape the field's outlook in the future.

(+) Decisive and courageous political action is needed in order to create the conditions and steering principles for positive change. Design for politics!

(+) Industry and design must be socially responsible actors. Design for new lifestyles!

⚠ The choice of lifestyle remains our own responsibility. Within a given framework, we must define for ourselves what hand luggage we take on our flight on spaceship earth. Design for society!

14

162 Tools for the Design Revolution

Tools for the Design Revolution 163

⑭ How Should We Live?

A tale of possibilities

The question "How can we lead responsible lives that limit the consequences of our lifestyle to a world-compatible level?" often receives knee-jerk answers, such as: it is the job of politicians to provide the guidelines; industry and its greed-generating marketing machine has to start first; if industrialized nations like the U.S. and China do not take the first steps, the decisions here in tiny Europe are only drops in the bucket, and so on.

It is always someone else – not ourselves; the legitimate doubting of whether or not an individual can even make a significant contribution to a positive change remains a convenient excuse. The responsibility can certainly be split into three areas: politics – industry – individuals. How then can each individual lead a socially and ecologically sustainable lifestyle?

And where do we start?
Numerous scientific findings have shown that humanity exerts a strong influence on the environment and transforms it to a large extent. Humans have long been a geological factor. A general acknowledgement of this would be an important step in the discussion on how to deal with the environment. The consumption areas of food and agriculture, mobility and tourism as well as housing and energy use in buildings are responsible for about eighty percent of all environmental impacts.

⚠ The aforementioned areas come with a variety of more or less poorly designed and rarely forward-looking artifacts, services and infrastructures – these represent design tasks!

⚠ These very areas – nutrition, mobility and housing – can be greatly affected by the individual customization of lifestyles!

One of the reasons for the immense growth of the environmental impact of our lifestyle is the dramatic increase in recent decades of the entitled attitude of the people. We are living beyond our means – and the means of our world.

Wie leben?

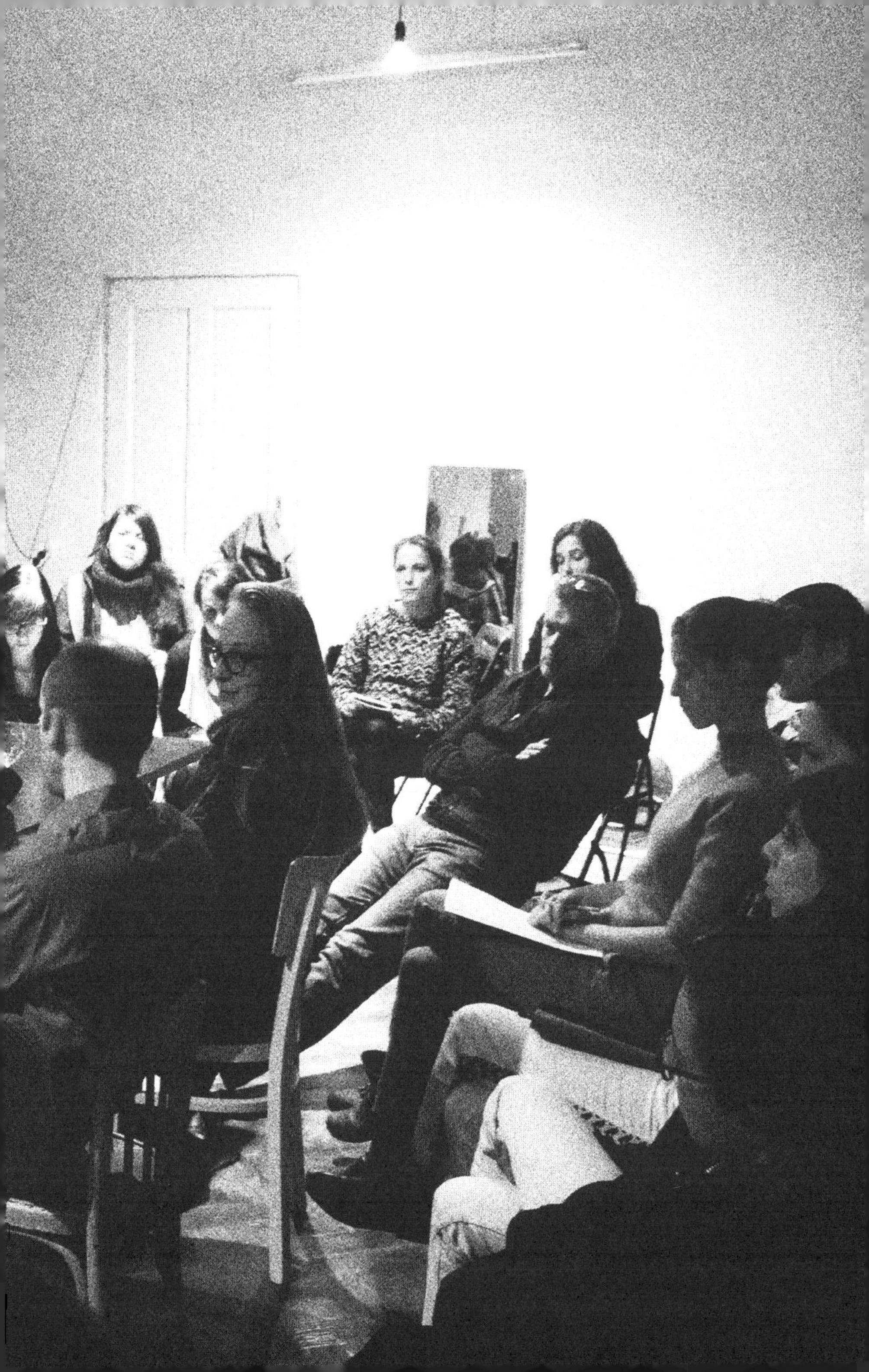

"We are in essence all children of this pyromaniacal age; we have grown accustomed to living with an unbelievably high level of daily waste. We have even internalised our 'right to waste things' and view that as the solid core of human rights."

Peter Sloterdijk (Feireiss 2010:212)

This is the current situation. Now we have two choices:

⚠ Continue to ignore the reality and eventually be painfully surprised that an estimated 97 percent of climate researchers and scientists have been right. Then all that remains is the task of explaining to the next generation why we ignored the available information at their expense.

⚠ We recognize the threat to our planet, our environment, our health and our future generations and say that the risk is too high; we have chosen a more conscientious, energy-saving and less resource-intensive life.

Approaches

We are used to relying on science, technology and design to solve our problems. For decades, we have shown that we can adapt the world to fit our needs. Accordingly, we have "calming" fantasies of omnipotence, in which one or another super technology in the coming decades will bring a happy change of direction in an exciting and wonderful future. Damage to the climate and planet will be – if not repaired – at least stopped in its tracks. In this century, we would even tap the energy of the stars, according to Michio Kaku. Nuclear fusion and magnetism will be the technical achievements that provide the required climate-neutral energy sources for our habitually expansive lifestyle.

⚠ If the belief in the technical solvability of the dramatic environmental changes of the past years cannot be redeemed, then the last climate change deniers and value relativists will need a Plan B.

Ideas or proposals for such a Plan B are already being tried by many initiatives, organizations and activists. Everywhere, something is in the air; it's stirring something in the system! (World Calculation Models ↗)

In addition, there are a number of individual activists experimenting on themselves in order to demonstrate the frivolity of our system – usually in ways that attract media attention. With their often symbolic acts (living a year without plastic, etc.) they encourage people to think. But the truly interesting thing is that these are people who do not agonize abstractly over what doesn't work, but instead gather experiences about what does work.

(+) Also, look for an experience-based research approach: try to modify areas of your own life through sustainable alternatives.

However, we must not forget that all the aforementioned ideas, approaches, initiatives and subcultures are inextricably linked to a world in which no one has to struggle for their very existence.

⚠ Alternatives can only arise where there is the possibility of discovering them; to question the status quo.
This makes our obligation to look for alternatives all the greater.

What makes a good life?

There is certainly no universal answer.
In our context, we mean lifestyles whose effects are as world-compatible and environmentally conscious as possible. By focusing on such basic principles as awareness, autonomy and self-determination for each individual, a new quality of life can be achieved. Autonomy and self-determination should not be mistaken for the neoliberal concept of freedom, however, which presupposes the absolute freedom of the markets and even becomes a battle cry of the bourgeois elites against the "powerless".

Other "basic goods" for a contented life include, for example: Health – as a value that enables free actions and decisions at the individual level. The side effects of modern life are often not conducive to health. Security – which implies protection from the hazards caused by the impacts of climate change as well as the reduction of social inequalities and with them, for example, future flows of refugees (including climate refugees). Respect – as understanding the viewpoints of others (and vice versa), it is a core value on the path to a future of global solidarity, and extends far beyond formal equality through civil and human rights!

Natural or environmental awareness is undisputedly an essential element of a sustainable life in our context. To live in harmony with something is not to manipulate it for your own purposes.

(+) Which values are associated with quality of life for you personally?

(+) Reconsider what you do for a healthy life. What world-compatible concepts of recreation are available? What influence does diet have?

(+) Take an interest in the production conditions for the foods and products you consume. Challenge companies to information transparency in this regard.

(+) The alienation from natural processes can be counteracted. Find out about local food cultivation and participate. How important is nature in your life?

We need a shift in values!
To really change things, even ethical consumption is not enough: The growth imperative of capitalism will continue by other means despite the contrary evidence of the finiteness of our world. Consuming the "right thing" does not alter the fact that, in the game of supply and demand, there are always those who cannot afford the market price. The fixation of our society on consumption and work stands massively in the way of a life based on solidarity and empathy. Through the reduction of consumer pressure, many constraints can be eliminated and spaces for development realized. Over the past decades, we have created many conveniences for ourselves and supposedly gained time. But where has that time gone?

Simplifying life can mean an immense gain in time and financial freedom. This also corresponds to models that, in addition to economic prosperity, involve, for example, time prosperity, activity prosperity, relationship prosperity or information prosperity as aspects of a meaningful life.

This shift of values automatically implies an exploration of the limits of comfort, but these limits do not have to be demolished. The concept of "ownership" can be replaced by offering shared use, for example.

(+) If I do not own everything I need in everyday life, what advantages arise from this?

(+) If I lose something, what do I gain?

⚠ To bring about a change in values, to break out of the matrix, we need to be critical and keep questioning things, identifying undesirable developments, and seeking out and implementing alternatives.

⚠ What new qualities open up through a focus on values instead of possessions?

And what does that have to do with design?
Design is always intertwined with social issues, phenomena and problems. Design operates in the midst of these fields, in the midst of society and its contradictions. As innovators of everyday culture, the consumer goods industry and product-service system providers, designers for all relevant fields can also think of sustainable solutions.

But apart from that:

⚠ Every designer is also, first and foremost, a citizen.

Let us not leave our world any longer to politicians, who are controlled by power and vested interests, profit-driven corporations and our own convenience.

The question "how should we live?" can be answered: consciously and self-determined, driven by critical thinking, gathering and questioning information.

A sustainable lifestyle begins with the personal behavior of every citizen. Like any citizens' movement, this initiative from below is only the beginning. In this way can the avalanche of alternative-acting "knowledge elites" begin to roll toward an effective movement encompassing the world's population. Then, finally, the actions of governments and corporations can no longer be divorced from the interests of informed citizens.

⚠ "How should we live?" can be seen as a symbolic question, to consider our own lifestyle in terms of its sustainability and to explore the new possibilities of a world-compatible life, in order to bring Spaceship Earth to a steady course.

Tools for the Design Revolution

15

⑮ Future Concepts

PPPP: Possible, Plausible, Preferable, Probable

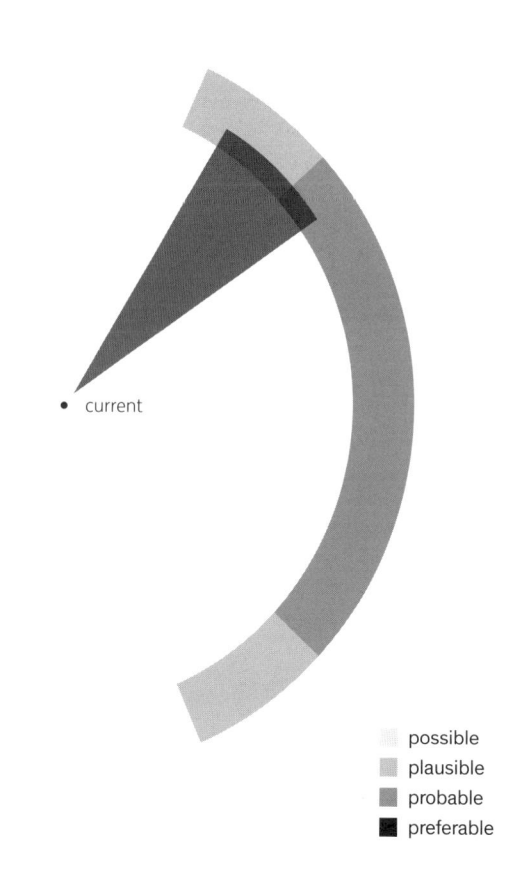

• current

possible
plausible
probable
preferable

Source: Fiona Raby, Anthony Dunne, 2014.5, based on Candy 2009 and Voros 2001

174   Tools for the Design Revolution

Future concepts

Given the urgent need to change the system, it is important to develop a large number of new realms of possibility. There are many paths to the future – not just one.

With their book *Speculative Everything. Design, Fiction and Social Dreaming*, Fiona Raby and Anthony Dunne presented a very striking tool that encourages the development of new solutions beyond the familiar – and the use of design to make them conceivable as well as negotiable for a large number of people. Innovation occurs not only through technological innovations, but also through the potential for radical social change. What is probable, plausible and possible should not be developed in isolation, but rather jointly in an interdisciplinary context. Each discipline, each individual already has the potential to make a significant contribution to possible developments today.

Alternatives

Today, the direction-setting parameters are still being decided at the intersection of business and politics, but also through consumer decisions and behaviors. Unfortunately, the entire scope of future developments is not being exploited at this intersection. The Design Revolution triggers positive change by exploring new scenarios! The assessment of what is possible through the development of new alternatives opens up a new horizon for models of a better future. What we need is the development, participation, documentation, discussion and freedom of choice of …

Alternatives

Alternatives

Alternatives

Alternatives

Alternatives

Alternatives

Alternatives

Alter

Alternatives

Alte

Alternatives

Alternatives

Alternatives

Alternatives

Alternatives

Alternatives

Alternatives

Glossary of Terms for Sustainable Design

Autonomy
To design products and services in such a way as to encourage people to be self-directed, rather than hindering it and creating dependencies.

Cascading
Chained temporal use phases. This means step-by-step use phases through different value creation levels in order to take advantage of products and systems for as long as possible until their disposal is unavoidable.

Cooperation
(Long Life ↗), p. 112

Deceleration
Taking things more slowly.

Dematerialization
The radical reduction of the use of natural material resources to meet human needs. Neither ecological nor economical sustainability works without dematerialization.

Design for Disassembly
If products can be disassembled, valuable raw materials such as aluminum are recyclable and can be reused – or used further, in the case of repairable products. The product should contain as few different material compounds as possible, the variety of screws used should be kept to a minimum and different materials should not be put togetherin such a way that they cannot be taken apart.

Design for Repair
To design products in such a way that individual parts can be replaced if they are worn and do not have to be completely discarded in case of damage. This requires a modular product design, the ability to disassemble the product, and the use of standardized components that are available as spare parts.

Durability
(Quick Death ↗), p. 96

Efficiency
Products and services that satisfy human needs and ensure a high quality of life while radically reducing the negative environmental impact and resource consumption to a minimum throughout their life cycle, so as not to overuse the Earth's natural capacity. (This concept is not meant economically here.)

Longevity
(Long Life ↗), p. 112
(Cofee Box ↗), p. 80

Modularity
A product and service design that makes it possible to expand or replace temporarily necessary or worn-out modules at will.

Open Culture
(Stimulants ↗), p. 32
(Quick Death ↗), p. 96

Recyclability
(Resurrection ↗), p. 122

Robustness / Resilience
Products or systems should be designed so that they are resistant to external disturbances.

Service-friendliness
(Long Life ↗), p. 112

Simplicity
Ensuring a simple product construction and a plan for minimal corporate hierarchies and direct distribution channels.

Small is beautiful
(Stimulants ↗), p. 32

Upcycling
(Resurrection ↗), p. 122

Usability
Intuitive use and optimized ergonomics. The person defines the product, and not vice versa.

"I believe that a desirable future depends … on our engendering a life style which will enable us to be spontaneous, independent, yet related to each other, rather than maintaining a life style which only allows us to make and unmake, produce and consume – a style of life which is merely a way station on the road to the depletion and pollution of the environment.

The future depends more upon our choice of institutions which support a life of action than on our developing new ideologies and technologies.

We need a set of criteria which will permit us to recognize those institutions which support personal growth rather than addiction […]"

Ivan Illich, 1971:52

References and Recommended Reading

For Gourmets

Christopher Alexander et al., *A Pattern Language*, 1977

Gui Bonsiepe, *Design im Übergang zum Sozialismus*, 1971–1973

Gui Bonsiepe, *Interface – An Approach to Design*, 1999 (original: *Dall'oggetto al interfaccia*, 1995)

Murray Bookchin, *Post Scarcity Anarchism*, 1971

Lucius Burckhardt, *Design der Zukunft*, 1988

Lucius Burckhardt, *Die Kinder fressen ihre Revolution*, 1993

John Cage, *Pour les oiseaux*, 1976

John Cage, *A Year from Monday*, 1968

Stéphane Hessel, *Time for Outrage!*, 2011

Julian Bicknell, Liz McQuiston (eds.), *Design for Need*, 1977

Wam Kat, *24 Rezepte zur kulinarischen Weltverbesserung*, 2008

Ed van Hinte, *Eternally Yours*, 1997

Magazines

agora 42, sustainability, 2012

Politische Ökologie, sustainable design, 2007

Starting Point

Stewart Brand (ed.), *The Whole Earth Catalog*, 1968

Howard Rheingold, *The Millennium Whole Earth Catalog*, Copyright © 1994 by Point Foundation. Reprinted by permission of HarperCollins Publishers. (Cover image pp. 8/9)

Global Tools, Edizioni L'uomo e l'arte, June 1974 (Cover image p. 10)

Further Reading

Diedrich Diederichsen, Anselm Franke (eds.), *The Whole Earth. California and the Disappearance of the Outside*, 2013

Marshall McLuhan, Quentin Fiore, *The Medium is the Massage*, 1967

1. A Global Issue

All of these sources are available free of charge on the Internet, where they are updated from time to time. The exact Internet addresses for the given documents and data are omitted here, because the documents are easier to find and more consistently available through search engines. Most importantly, the updated versions of these reports and data should be accessed in order to create an informed picture of the situation in the world.

Institutions

Global Footprint Network, www.globalfootprintnetwork.org

International Energy Agency (IEA), www.iea.org

Intergovernmental Panel on Climate Change (IPCC), www.ipcc.ch

United Nations Development Program (UNDP), www.undp.org
United Nations, Department of Economic and Social Affairs, Population division (UN), www.unpopulation.org

United Nations Environment Programme
(UNEP), www.unep.org

2,000-watt society, www.2000watt.ch

References

City of Zurich, *On the Way to the 2,000-Watt Society. Zurich's Path to Sustainable Energy Use*, 2011

Jesko Fezer, Martin Schmitz (eds.): *Lucius Burckhardt. Wer plant die Planung? Architektur, Politik und Mensch*, 2004

IEA, Intergovernmental Panel on Climate Change: Key World Energy Statistics

Ivan Illich [1973], *Tools for Conviviality*, 1998

IPCC, "Summary for Policymakers", in: *Climate Change 2013: The Physical Science Basis*. Contribution of Working Group I to the Fifth Assessment Report of the Intergovernmental Panel on Climate Change [Stocker, T. F., D. Qin, G.-K. Plattner, M. Tignor, S. K. Allen, J. Boschung, A. Nauels, Y. Xia, V. Bex and P. M. Midgley (eds.)], 2013

One Tonne Life, *Final Report*, www.onetonnelife.se

Rajenda Kumar Pachauri, *Conclusions of the IPCC Working Group I Fifth Assessment Report*, AR4, SREX and SRREN. Lecture at the climate conference in Warsaw, Poland, 13.11.13

Williams E. Rees, Mathis Wackernagel et al., *Our Ecological Footprint*, 1998

Mathis Wackernagel, Bert Beyers, *Der Ecological Footprint*, 2013

Mathis Wackernagel, William Rees, *Our Ecological Footprint. Reducing Human Impact on the Earth*, 2013
UN Department of Economic and Social Affairs, *Population Division: World Population 2012* (Wallchart), 2013

UNDP, *Human Development Report 2013. The Rise of the South: Human Progress in a Diverse World*, 2013

UNEP, *A New Angle on Sovereign Credit Risk. E-RISC: Environmental Risk Integration in Sovereign Credit Analysis*, Phase 1 Report, 2012

Wolfgang Sachs et al., *Fair Future: Resource Conflicts, Security and Global Justice*, 2007

Footprint Calculator

Footprint Network (in multiple languages), www.footprintnetwork.org/en/index.php/GFN/page/calculators

2. Stimulants

Frithjof Bergmann, Stephan Schumacher, *Neue Arbeit, neue Kultur*, 2008

R. Buckminster Fuller [1969], *Operating Manual for Spaceship Earth*, 2008

Foundation Earth, *Rethinking Society from the Ground Up. A Foundation Earth working paper on a new economic model*, 2012, www.fdnearth.org

Yona Friedman, *Utopies réalisables*, 1975

Wolfgang Haug, *Critique of Commodity Aesthetics*, 1986 (original: *Kritik der Warenästhetik*, 1971)

Rob Hopkins, *The Transition Town Handbook. From oil dependency to local resilience*, 2009

Rob Hopkins, *The transition companion. Making your community more resilient in uncertain times*, 2011

Ivan Illich [1973], *Tools for Conviviality*, 1998

Tim Jackson, *Prosperity Without Growth: Economics for a Finite Planet*, 2009

William Morris [1891], *News from Nowhere*, 1991

E. F. Schumacher [1973], *Small is Beautiful. A Study of Economics as if People Mattered*, 1993

John Thackara, *In the Bubble. Designing in a Complex World*, 2005

John Thackara, *True Cost Design – In Three Steps*, 2010: www.doorsofperception.com/learning-institutions/true-cost-design-in-three-steps

Henry David Thoreau [1854], *Walden. Or, Life in the Woods*, 2008

Ursula Tischner, Carlo Vezzoli, *Sustainability Evaluation Radars*, 2009

Bas van Abel et al., *Open Design Now*, 2011

Websites

Buckminster Fuller Institute, www.bfi.org

Creative Commons, www.creativecommons.org

New Work Homepage, www.newworknewculture.com

New Work movement, www.neuearbeit-neuekultur.de

Open Design Foundation, www.opendesign.org

Further Reading

Ugo Bardi, *Extracted*, 2014

Rachel Carson [1963], *Silent Spring*, 2002

Al Gore, *An Inconvenient Truth*, 2006

Joachim Krausse, *Your Private Sky: R. Buckminster Fuller*, 1999

Annie Leonard, *The Story of Stuff*, 2010

Le Monde Diplomatique, *Atlas der Globalisierung*, 2012

Bruce Mau, *Massive Change*, 2004

Donella H. Meadows, Jorgen Randers et al., *The Limits to Growth*, 1974

Victor Papanek, *Design for the Real World*, 1971

Gunter Pauli, *The Blue Economy*, 2010

Jorgen Randers, *2052: A Global Forecast for the Next Forty Years*, 2012

Cynthia Smith, *Design for the Other 90%*, 2007

Alex Steffen, *Worldchanging*, 2008

Ernst Ulrich von Weizsäcker et al., *Factor Five*, 2009

3. Recipes

Graphic (resources of an average German): Oekom Verlag (ed.), *Rohstoffquelle Abfall: Wie aus Müll Produkte von morgen werden*, 2012

EPD Arper Catifa: epd-norge.no NEPD Nr.: 102D 2009

EPD Barilla: Barilla, CPC code 2371, PCR 2010, S-P-00217: Environmental Product Declaration of durum wheat semolina dried pasta in paperboard box, world.

4. Life Cycle Analysis

European Commission – Life Cycle Thinking and Assessment, http://eplca.jrc.ec.europa.eu

Memorandum Product Carbon Footprint Position statement on measurement and communication of the product carbon footprint for international standardization and harmonization purposes, www.bmu.de

ProBas – Material Database on Environmental Impacts, www.probas.umweltbundesamt.de

Merel Segers, Joost Vogtländer, *Fast Track LCA*, www.ecocostsvalue.com

Stiftung Initiative Mehrweg, www.stiftung-mehrweg.de

Joost Vogtländer, *LCA, a practical guide for students, designers and business managers*, 2012, www.vssd.nl/hlf/b018.htm

Software

We have no examples to cite here, as we have so far only found profit-oriented versions.

5. Universal Tools

PE International, GaBi LCA software
IPCC, Carbon Dioxide Intensity of Electricity, www.ipcc.ch/pdf/special-reports/sroc/Tables/t0305.pdf, March 2014

Apple, Environmental Report, iPhone 5S and MacBook Pro 15", 2013

Mercedes Benz, Life Cycle – Environmental Certification M-Class, 2012
Volkswagen, Environmental Commendation Golf VIII, 2012 and e-Up, 2013

6. Coffee Box

Harald Gruendl, "Kommt's nur auf die Crema an?", *Spectrum* IX, insert to *Die Presse*, 14 December 2013

Rajenda Kumar Pachauri, *Conclusions of the IPCC Working Group I Fifth Assessment Report*, AR4, SREX and SRREN. Lecture at the climate conference in Warsaw, Poland, 13 November 2013

7. Quick Death

Cosima Dannoritzer, Jürgen Reuß, *Kaufen für die Müllhalde. Das Prinzip der geplanten Obsoleszenz*, Freiburg 2012

Christian Kreiß, Stefan Schridde, *Geplante Obsoleszenz, Gutachten im Auftrag der Bundestagsfraktion Bündnis 90*, Die Grünen, 2012; available online

Giles Slade, *Made to Break: Technology and Obsolescence in America*, 2007

Websites

Amnesty International on the AK-47, www.amnesty.org, 2006

Ifixit, The free repair guide for everything, written by everyone, www.ifixit.com

Make: Technology on your time, makezine.com

Murks? Nein danke! (Botch-up? No Thanks!), www.murks-nein-danke.de

Reparatur- und Service-Zentrum (Repair and Service Center), Vienna www.rusz.at

9. Resurrection

Michael Braungart, William McDonough, *Cradle to Cradle: Remaking the Way We Make Things*, 2002

Ernest Dichter [1971], *Überzeugen, nicht verführen. Die Kunst, Menschen zu beeinflussen*, 1985

MBDC, Summary of Cradle to Cradle®
Certification Criteria, 2009, www.mbdc.com

Water Footprint Network, www.waterfootprint.org

10. Greenwashing

Ecolabel Index, *Who is deciding what's green?*, www.ecolabelindex.com/ecolabels

Plötzlich sind alle Klimaretter. Wirklich?, www.klima-luegendetektor.de

The Sins of Greenwashing, sinsofgreenwashing.org

11. Creativity Tools

Bernhard Dusch, *Sustainable Design Matrix* 2013

Wilfried Konrad et al., *Das nachhaltige Büro*, 2003

Carlo Vezzoli, Ezio Manzini, *Design for environmental sustainability*, 2008

Manifestos

Allan Chochinov, *1000 Words: A Manifesto for Sustainability in Design*, www.core77.com

Ken Garland with 20 other designers, *first things first*, 1964, www.designishistory.com

William McDonough, *The Hannover Principles*, www.mcdonough.com
Manifesto on processes of change, www.intrastructures.net

Slow Design Principles, www.slowlab.net

Association of German Industrial Designers, *Der VDID Codex Industriedesign*, www.vdid.de

The Ecological Oath: The Hippocratic Oath for Designers, www.oekologischer-eid.de

www.alliance-francaise-des-designers.org, AFD Charter for Eco-Designers, 2014

Guidelines and Checklists

A420, *An Introductory Guide to Sustainability for Designers, Financial + Social + Environmental + Personal = Sustainable*, www.a420.com

Bootcamp bootleg; Hasso Plattner, Institute of Design at Stanford, www.dschool.stanford.edu

Cooper-Hewitt, National Design Museum, *Design and Social Impact*, www.cooperhewitt.org

Integration Ecological Design, Okala Practitioner; Industrial Designers Society of America (IDSA), www.okala.net

German Federal Ecodesign Award, criteria matrix, www.bundespreis-ecodesign.de

The Living Principles, Scorecard, www.livingprinciples.org

The Designer's Field Guide to Sustainability; Lunar, www.lunar.com

Guideline and Check List Manual for the Design of Low Impact Products for the Environment; RAPI.labo, Milano, www.lens-italia.polimi.it

Angie Rattay, *Planet Earth – Directions for Use*, 2011

Summary of Cradle to Cradle Certification Criteria, ww.c2ccertified.org

John Thackara, *True Cost Design*, Handouts and lists, www.doorsofperception.com

Ursula Tischner, Carlo Vezzoli, *Sustainability Design-Orienting Toolkit (SDO)*, www.sdo-lens.polimi.it

Ursula Tischer, Carlo Vezzoli, "Sustainability Evaluation Radars" (see UNEP/TU Delft 2009, DfS Product Service Systems worksheets), in: *Design for Sustainability: A Step by Step Approach*, UNEP, TU Delft 2009, www.d4s-sbs.org

toolkit wiki: Dan Lockton, *Design with Intent*, www.danlockton.com

Fiona Raby, Anthony Dunne, *Work in progress (a) (b)*, 2009, www.dunneandraby.co.uk

Strategic Tools

Cambridge Sustainable Design Toolkit (University of Cambridge), www.cambridge-sustainable-design-toolkit.com

Design Play Cards (eco-innovators)

Drivers of change (A.R.U.P.)

Flowmaker – a Design tool (wemake)

Lego, Serious Play (other blocks in general)

Mind the Future (W.I.R.E), www.mindthefuture.net

Open Design Now, www.opendesignnow.org

Rethink (rethink games ltd), www.playrethink.com

SIS-Toolkit (OVAM)

Emily Pilloton, Jince Kuruvilla: *Design Revolution. The Toolkit*, 2009

Tools for Calculating the Environmental Impact of Materials

Energy Trumps (The agency of design), www.agencyofdesign.co.uk

Ecolizer 2.0 (OVAM), www.ecodesignlink.be/en

Water footprint (virtual water), www.virtualwater.eu

12. Offending the Audience

The play *Publikumsbeschimpfung (Offending the Audience)* by Peter Handke dates from the year 1965. The stage is empty; the auditorium and the stage are brightly lit. A reflection on the ideas, expectations and the ritual embeddedness of the audience unfolds. The design insults given here, inspired by Handke's style, come from the following sources:

Gui Bonsiepe, *interface – Design neu begreifen*, 1996:126 (original: *Dall'oggetto al interfaccia*, 1995)

Gui Bonsiepe, *Design im Übergang zum Sozialismus. Ein technisch-politischer Erfahrungsbericht aus dem Chile der Unidad Popular*, 1971–1973:16f.

Lucius Burckhardt [1980], "Design ist unsichtbar", in: Jesko Fezer, Martin Schmitz (eds.): *Lucius Burckhardt. Wer plant die Planung? Architektur, Politik und Mensch*, 2004:188ff.

John Cage, *A Year from Monday*, 1975:8; Cage gave the lecture "Diary: How to Improve the World (You will only make matters worse)" at an international design conference in Aspen.

R. Buckminster Fuller, *Operating Manual for Spaceship Earth*, 1969

Peter Handke [1966], *Publikumsbeschimpfung und andere Sprechstücke*, 2012:13

Tomás Maldonado, *Design, Nature & Revolution*, 1972:11 (original: *La speranza progettuale*, 1970)

Victor Papanek [1971], *Design for the Real World*, 1997:ix

The two last insults come from designers who once contributed to the aforementioned problems through their work in major international design studios. Perhaps we are now finally entering an era of repentance?

Tim Brown, *Change by Design*, 2009:193

Hartmut Esslinger, *Schwungrat: Wie Design-Strategien die Zukunft der Wirtschaft gestalten*, 2009:123f

13. A Personal Matter

John Thackara, *In the Bubble. Designing in a Complex World*, 2005

Further Reading

Tim Brown, *Change by Design*, 2009

Edward Datschefski, *The Total Beauty of Sustainable Products*, 2001

Alastair Fuad-Luke, *Design Activism: Beautiful Strangeness for a Sustainable World*, 2009

Ezio Manzini, Carlo Vezzoli, *Design for Environmental Sustainability*, 2010

Paul Micklethwaite, Anne Chick, *Design for Sustainable Change*, 2011

Emily Pilloton, *Design Revolution*, 2009

Nathan Shedroff, *Design is the Problem*, 2009

Ursula Tischner et al., *How to Do Ecodesign?*, 2000

Friedrich von Borries et al., *Klimakunstforschung*, 2011

Stuart Walker, *Sustainable by Design*, 2006

14. How Should We Live?

Paul J. Crutzen et al., *Das Raumschiff Erde hat keinen Notausgang. Energie und Politik im Anthropozän*, 2011

Hans Holzinger, *Neuer Wohlstand. Leben und Wirtschaften auf einem begrenzten Planeten*, 2012

Michio Kaku, *Physics of the Future: The Inventions That Will Transform Our Lives*, 2012

Robert Jacob, Alexander Skidelsky et al. [2012], *Wie viel ist genug? Vom Wachstumswahn zu einer Ökonomie des guten Lebens*, 2013

Lukas Feireiss, *Gebäude sind Partner ihrer Bewohner, Der Philosoph Peter Sloterdijk im Gespräch mit dem Kurator Lukas Feireiss*, 2010

Further Reading

Friedrich Schmidt-Bleek, Klaus Wiegandt, *Nutzen wir die Erde richtig?*, 2008

15. Future Concepts

Fiona Raby, Anthony Dunne, *Speculative Everything: Design, Fiction, and Social Dreaming*, 2014

Stuart Candy, *Presentation of Potencial Futures*, Design Interactions Program at Royal Collage of Art, 2009

Joseph Voros, *A Primer on Futures Studies, Foresight and the Use of Scenarios*, 2001 www.thinkingfutures.net

Ivan Illich, *Deschooling Society*, 1971, http://www.preservenet.com/theory/Illich/Deschooling/chap4.html

List of Illustrations of the IDRV's Activities

p. 27

Dymaxion World
View of the Dymaxion World Map by R. Buckminster Fuller, from the *Werkzeuge für die Design-Revolution* (*Tools for the Design Revolution*) exhibition by the IDRV at Designmonat Graz, 2013

pp. 46/47

The Consequences of Design
(installation view)
An intervention by the IDRV in collaboration with the Cologne International School of Design (KISD) at the imm cologne furniture fair, 2013

p. 54

Rein in die weißen Kittel!
(Put on the white coat!)
The agents in the Design Revolution, 2014

pp. 68/69

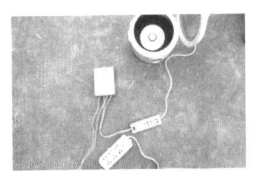

Workshop: Werkzeuge für die Design-Revolution (Tools for the Design Revolution)
Application of the universal tools with students at the Southwest Jiaotong University, Chengdu, 2012

pp. 100/101

Kaufen für den Mistplatz
(Buying for the Dump)
IDRV field research at the Zehetnergasse dump site, Vienna, 2009

p. 119

Im Radlager (At Radlager)
IDRV field research for the project *Haben wir das Zeug dazu?* (*Do we have what it takes?*) as part of Vienna Design Week, 2013

p. 120

Beim Geigenbaumeister Schueler (At Schueler's Luthier Shop)
IDRV field research for the project *Haben wir das Zeug dazu?* (*Do we have what it takes?*) as part of Vienna Design Week, 2013

p. 158

Start the Design Revolution
(installation view)
Personal protest signs in the *Werkzeuge für die Design-Revolution* (*Tools for the Design Revolution*) exhibition by the IDRV for Designmonat Graz, 2013

pp. 162/163

Weltmahlzeit (World Meal)
A meat, fish or vegan meal, each corresponding to a combined value of 2.7 kg CO_2-eq per day. For the vegan lunch, this amounted to 1.2 kg of lentils; the fish dish with vegetables added up to 0.35 kg on the plate and the beef stew with bread 0.07 kg. *World Meal* workshop by Harald Gruendl at the University of Applied Arts Vienna, 2014

pp. 166/167

Circle 00007 (r=4): How Should We Live? The Art of Sustainable Living
A panel discussion with Christoph Breuer (KAIROS impact research and development gGmbH), Nunu Knaller (activist, blogger), Maren Richter (curator, critic) and Harald Gruendl (IDRV head, designer), at pataform, Vienna 2013

Agents in Tools for the Design Revolution

IDRV – Institute of Design Research Vienna, a non-profit organization, is making an independent academic contribution to the establishment of design science. Since its foundation in 2008 by Harald Gruendl, this extra-university institute has worked on interdisciplinary strategies of knowledge production and mediation, and focuses on research in the areas of sustainable design and design history. www.idrv.org

Harald Gruendl (*1967)
studied industrial design at the University of Applied Arts Vienna and co-founded the studio EOOS in 1995 with Martin Bergmann and Gernot Bohmann. He completed his postgraduate studies with a Ph.D. in 2005 and a habilitation in 2009 on the theory and history of design.

Ulrike Haele (*1972)
studied journalism/communications and political science at the University of Vienna. In parallel, she completed her industrial design studies at the University of Applied Arts Vienna. She works in the spaces between these disciplines and is a research fellow at the IDRV.

Marco Kellhammer (*1988)
studied industrial design at the University of Applied Science of Osnabrück and deals with the subjects of ethics and ecology in design. This has continued in his work as a research assistant at the IDRV, where he conducts research on the topic of sustainable development.

Christina Nägele (*1976)
studied cultural studies and aesthetic practice at the University of Hildesheim. She works at the intersection of visual art, architecture and design in the areas of curatorial practice, cultural transmission and communication.

grafisches büro
was founded in 2003, on the basis of the shared work of Günter Eder and Roman Breier, in 2006 Marcel Neundörfer joined the partnership. The main focus of their work is the development of visual identities in an intermedia context.

Imprint

This publication is a follow-up project from the IDRV's *Tools for the Design Revolution* exhibition, which was developed in 2012 in cooperation with designaustria for designforum Vienna and presented in 2013 at designforum Vorarlberg and Designmonat Graz.

Editors:
IDRV – Institute of Design Research Vienna,
Harald Gruendl, Marco Kellhammer,
Christina Nägele
www.idrv.org

Authors: Harald Gruendl, Ulrike Haele, Marco Kellhammer, Christina Nägele

Conception and editing: Harald Gruendl, Marco Kellhammer, Christina Nägele

Research assistants: Alexandra Bischof, Bernhard Ranner

Interns: Ronja Ullrich, Pia Plankensteiner

Copy editing: Christina Bösel, Textschiff

Translation: Jason S. Heilman

Photos: Chantal Bavaud, p. 54
Stephan Friesinger, p. 27
Felix Groefler, pp. 10–15, 32–44, 70, 76, 122f., 140–145, 162f.
Paul Wimmer, pp. 4–9, 18f., 48, 64f., 80–97, 105–108, 112–117, 124–130, 137f., 149
all others: IDRV

Layout: grafisches Büro, Vienna

Printing: gugler, Melk
PEFC 70%, C2C

Paper: Pureprint 01

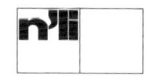

© 2014 by niggli Verlag, Sulgen
www.niggli.ch
ISBN 978-3-7212-0903-7

© 2014, IDRV – Institute of Design Research Vienna, the authors and photographers

Unless otherwise stated, any potential use of the entire text is governed by Creative Commons: Attribution-NonCommercial-ShareAlike 3.0 Unported License: creativecommons.org/licenses/by-nc-sa/3.0

This publication is also available in German as ISBN 978-3-7212-0902-0.

Made possible through the support of:

BUNDESKANZLERAMT ÖSTERREICH
KUNST

lebensministerium.at

departure
Die Kreativagentur
der Stadt Wien

Thanks for the support and the knowledge sharing of: Helmut Antrekovitsch, Linus Baumschlager, Martin Bergmann, Markus Böhm, Gernot Bohmann, breadedEscalope, DANKLHAMPEL, designforum Graz, designforum Vorarlberg, designforum Wien, Severin Filek, Martina Fineder, Sebastian Gann, Günter Haider, Frederik Hedenus, André Hernâni, Magdalena Höller, Günter Horntrich, Sébastien Humbert, Dieter Hundstorfer, Albin Kälin, KAIROS Bregenz, Klasse Oliver Kartak, Renate and Ariane Kromp, Museum of Applied Art Vienna, Ezio Manzini, Martina Mara, Manfred Reichelt, Roland Schueler, Spirit Design, Roland Stulz, Christian Teckert, Arnold Teischinger, Ursula Tischner, Carlo Vezzoli, Vienna Design Week, Andrea Wiegelmann, Wolfgang Wimmer, Julia Zimmermann, ZIT – Technology Agency of the City of Vienna. And special thanks to the team from EOOS!